Vietnam War Crimes

Other books in the At Issue in History series:

Vietnam War Crimes

Samuel Brenner, *Book Editor*

Bruce Glassman, *Vice President*
Bonnie Szumski, *Publisher*
Helen Cothran, *Managing Editor*
Scott Barbour, *Series Editor*

 **AT ISSUE IN HISTORY**

GREENHAVEN PRESS
An imprint of Thomson Gale, a part of The Thomson Corporation

Detroit • New York • San Francisco • San Diego • New Haven, Conn.
Waterville, Maine • London • Munich

LIBRARY OF CONGRESS CATALOGING-IN-PUBLICATION DATA

Vietnam war crimes / Samuel Brenner, book editor.
   p. cm. — (At issue in history)
  Includes bibliographical references and index.
  ISBN 0-7377-2689-X (lib. bdg. : alk. paper)
   1. Vietnamese Conflict, 1961–1975—Atrocities. 2. War crimes. I. Brenner, Samuel. II. Series.
  DS559.2.V6 2006
  959.704'38—dc22
                                                2005046149

Contents

Chapter 2: The My Lai Massacre

Chapter 3: Vietnamese War Crimes

A left-wing academic suggests that reports that the North Vietnamese massacred political opponents during the Tet Offensive were manufactured by American agents who wanted to discredit the Vietnamese Communists.

Foreword

Historian Robert Weiss defines history simply as "a record and interpretation of past events." Both elements—record and interpretation—are necessary, Weiss argues.

> Names, dates, places, and events are the essence of history. But historical writing is not a compendium of facts. It consists of facts placed in a sequence to tell a connected story. A work of history is not merely a story, however. It also must analyze what happened and *why*—that is, it must interpret the past for the reader.

For example, the events of December 7, 1941, that led President Franklin D. Roosevelt to call it "a date which will live in infamy" are fairly well known and straightforward. A force of Japanese planes and submarines launched a torpedo and bombing attack on American military targets in Pearl Harbor, Hawaii. The surprise assault sank five battleships, disabled or sank fourteen additional ships, and left almost twenty-four hundred American soldiers and sailors dead. On the following day, the United States formally entered World War II when Congress declared war on Japan.

These facts and consequences were almost immediately communicated to the American people who heard reports about Pearl Harbor and President Roosevelt's response on the radio. All realized that this was an important and pivotal event in American and world history. Yet the news from Pearl Harbor raised many unanswered questions. Why did Japan decide to launch such an offensive? Why were the attackers so successful in catching America by surprise? What did the attack reveal about the two nations, their people, and their leadership? What were its causes, and what were its effects? Political leaders, academic historians, and students look to learn the basic facts of historical events and to read the intepretations of these events by many different sources, both primary and secondary, in order to develop a more complete picture of the event in a historical context.

In the case of Pearl Harbor, several important questions surrounding the event remain in dispute, most notably the role of President Roosevelt. Some historians have blamed his policies for deliberately provoking Japan to attack in order to propel America into World War II; a few have gone so far as to accuse him of knowing of the impending attack but not informing others. Other historians, examining the same event, have exonerated the president of such charges, arguing that the historical evidence does not support such a theory.

The Greenhaven At Issue in History series recognizes that many important historical events have been interpreted differently and in some cases remain shrouded in controversy. Each volume features a collection of articles that focus on a topic that has sparked controversy among eyewitnesses, contemporary observers, and historians. An introductory essay sets the stage for each topic by presenting background and context. Several chapters then examine different facets of the subject at hand with readings chosen for their diversity of opinion. Each selection is preceded by a summary of the author's main points and conclusions. A bibliography is included for those students interested in pursuing further research. An annotated table of contents and thorough index help readers to quickly locate material of interest. Taken together, the contents of each of the volumes in the Greenhaven At Issue in History series will help students become more discriminating and thoughtful readers of history.

Introduction

On a dark night in February 1969, a team of camouflaged men—a "special actions" team from Delta Platoon, SEAL Team One, Fire Team Bravo—under the command of twenty-five-year-old Lieutenant Bob Kerrey slipped into position around the Vietnamese village of Thanh Phong, a rural hamlet home to between 75 and 150 Vietnamese. Kerrey and his team were looking for the village secretary, or mayor, of Thanh Phong, who they believed was secretly meeting with a Vietcong military leader. The full story of what happened that night may never be known, but what is clear is that by the end of the evening a number of Vietnamese villagers, including many unarmed women and children, were dead: some with their throats cut and some shot while grouped together in the open. According to the stories told many years later both by a member of Kerrey's team and by a Vietnamese woman who says she was present that night, Kerrey ordered his men to execute civilians that they had taken prisoner. Kerrey himself and five other members of his team strongly dispute this version of events: According to them, the SEAL team was fired upon by Vietcong insurgents and returned fire into the darkness, killing the women and children by accident. "Please understand," Kerrey, then a U.S. senator from Nebraska, told a reporter from the *New York Times* in December 2000, "that my memory of this event is clouded by the fog of the evening, age and desire."[1]

The Thanh Phong incident, and Kerrey's role in whatever happened, remained largely secret until the story was broken in 2001 by a writer for the *New York Times Magazine*. Publication of this article immediately launched a firestorm of debate. Much of the debate was politically motivated: Kerrey, a very popular Democratic senator, had run for president in 1992 and was considering a second run in 2000. Once the story broke, some right-wing columnists (many of whom ordinarily praised what the United States had done in Vietnam) attacked Kerrey's version of events. They argued that the fact that a number of the dead women and children had been found huddled together outdoors indicated that they had been rounded up and executed. Other pundits and columnists, many of whom were left-wing and were ordinarily critical of U.S. actions in Vietnam, retorted by arguing that even if the article's version of events was correct, the circumstances of the war in Vietnam and the policies of the United States justified Kerrey's actions. He had simply done what he thought was necessary to protect his team in a hostile environment.

The furious political and public response to the reporting of the Thanh Phong incident, even three decades after the event itself had taken place, demonstrates the difficulty that Americans have in facing and answering questions about war crimes and atrocities in Vietnam. When the story broke, many Americans clearly felt that the *New York Times* was improperly raising topics that would have been better left buried. Mark Shields, a commentator on the *NewsHour with Jim Lehrer*, criticized the *New York Times* editorial about Thanh Phong (in which the *Times* editors suggested that Americans perhaps should question Kerrey's version of events) as "an act of moral arrogance rarely seen."[2] Kerrey himself went so far as to suggest that those reporting the story, rather than engaging in a necessary inquiry into what Americans had done in Vietnam, were actually attempting to attack the United States. "The Vietnam government likes to routinely say how terrible Americans were," Kerrey told the Associated Press. "The *Times* and CBS are now collaborating in that effort."[3] Other Americans felt that the problem was not that news outlets were investigating the story, but rather just the opposite: that news organizations were ignoring the story and were instead concentrating on more lurid political scandals. Some of these critics felt that by ignoring what had happened in Vietnam, Americans were losing the moral high ground in contemporary debates about war crimes and human rights. "The United States," wrote Jonathan Schell in the *Nation*, "cannot condemn in others what it covers up when committed by its own."[4]

The difficulty Americans have with discussing war crimes in Vietnam is perhaps due in part to the shame that many Americans feel about the war—shame over the things that American soldiers sometimes did in Vietnam, over how some Americans at home mistreated and abandoned those fighting in the name of the United States, or over how the

United States ultimately pulled out of Southeast Asia. The shame and anger about the war felt by all sides, however, does not by itself fully explain why Americans continue to struggle with questions about war crimes in Vietnam. Even today the subject of war crimes and atrocities in Vietnam remains enormously complicated and controversial, partly because of the still unclear nature of international law, partly because of uncertainty over exactly what happened in what was a confused and "dirty" conflict, and partly because of confusion over whether the official policies and strategies of the United States themselves constituted war crimes.

International Law and the Definition of "War Crimes"

The first problem with understanding or discussing the issue of war crimes in the Vietnam conflict is the uncertain definition of "war crimes" and the unsettled nature of international law. On the one hand, atrocities such as rape, torture, and murder are often easy to identify, but on the other hand, the term "war crimes" is meaningless without clear definition in legal codes. In order to be a crime, something must be against the law—and so in order for one nation to have committed crimes against another, or for the soldiers of one nation to have committed crimes against the soldiers of another, the actions committed by the nation or its soldiers must be against either international law or the laws of the individual nations involved.

The problem is that there is very little international law: While the United Nations often functions as if it were an international government, unlike a real government the United Nations has no sovereignty and no real capacity to act on its own. "International law" is thus composed of laws agreed to by individual states, usually after the drafting of international treaties. Sometimes these treaties or agreements are suggested by the United Nations, and sometimes they are proposed and negotiated by smaller groups of nations. Individual nations often pass national laws that differ in language from the laws suggested by the United Nations, thus creating a situation in which different nations have very different laws and definitions for the same crimes.

International legislation about war crimes was definitely in existence at the time of the Vietnam conflict. Modern international war crimes laws—which are generally said to be valid "according to the Geneva Convention"—date back to 1864, when under the urging of Henri Dunant, founder of the Red Cross, a number of nations signed the first Geneva Convention governing treatment of the sick and wounded in wartime. In fact, there is no single "Geneva Convention": The laws governing the wartime conduct of nations are laid out in a number of different agreements signed at various times during the nineteenth and twentieth centuries. Among the many Geneva Conventions, for instance, were 1899 treaties dealing with asphyxiating gases and expanding bullets; the 1925 Geneva Gas Protocol, which outlawed the use of poison gas and the practice of bacteriological warfare; and 1929 treaties on treatment of the wounded and prisoners of war.

Perhaps the most important Geneva Conventions in terms of regulating modern conflicts are the four treaties agreed to in 1949, in the wake of the Second World War and at the beginning of the Cold War. Of these agreements, two were on the treatment of wounded and sick soldiers and one was on the treatment of prisoners of war. The modern definition of war crimes was largely laid out in the fourth agreement, The Geneva Convention (IV) Relative to the Protection of Civilian Persons in Time of War. According to this convention—to which the United States was a signatory, and which the United States ratified in 1955—war crimes are defined as follows:

> Grave breaches . . . shall be those involving any of the following acts, if committed against persons or property protected by the present Convention: wilful killing, torture or inhuman treatment, including biological experiments, wilfully causing great suffering or serious injury to body or health unlawful deportation or transfer or unlawful confinement of a protected person, compelling a protected person to serve in the forces of a hostile Power, or wilfully depriving a protected person of the rights of fair and regular trial prescribed in the present Convention, taking of hostages and extensive destruction and appropriation of property, not justified by military necessity and carried out unlawfully and wantonly.[5]

The 1949 definition of war crimes seems clear. During the Vietnam conflict, however, it was not always easy to determine whether particular actions were or were not against international law. The issue was further complicated in Vietnam because the United States did not recognize North Vietnam as a sovereign nation, and thus some of the laws about conduct between nations were not applicable. Laws governing treatment of the Vietcong were even more complicated because the Vietcong insurgents were actually citizens of South Vietnam and not soldiers of North Vietnam. According to international law, they were therefore governed by the laws of South Vietnam rather than by any particular international war crimes legislation. The most serious question for Americans, however, became how to distinguish war crimes and atrocities from legitimate military actions.

A Dirty War

A second problem with facing the issue of war crimes in Vietnam is the nature of the Vietnam conflict itself. If, as the historian and journalist Studs Terkel has argued about World War II, there can be a "good" war, then Vietnam was by any definition a "bad" or a dirty war. Unlike in World War II, when the United States faced a vile and dangerous enemy and had a clear understanding of what it meant to win the war, in Vietnam the United States was fighting an invisible enemy and had no real sense of what victory looked like. As Myra MacPherson explains in *Long Time Passing: Vietnam and the Haunted Generation*, "A brutal disregard for civilians was woven into the war tactics in Vietnam—where the enemy was so indistinguishable from the innocent."[6] The United States, which had prepared its soldiers to fight the Soviets on the plains of Europe, was not prepared to fight a desperate guerrilla war for "the hearts and minds" of the Vietnamese people. The North Vietnamese and the Vietcong, who had already been struggling against the French for many years before fighting the United States and its South Vietnamese allies, had little patience and no sympathy for their enemies or those civilians who refused to support the Communist cause.

In Vietnam American soldiers were constantly faced with danger from seemingly innocent sources, including pregnant women, old men, and children. American soldiers would provide medical aid to South Vietnamese families and then find that those to whom they had provided aid had been tortured and executed as punishment for consorting with the Americans; the United States would give food to residents of impoverished hamlets and then find that that food was being used to feed Vietcong forces attacking American positions. It was often impossible for U.S. forces to determine who was dangerous and who was not, and so American soldiers tended to err on the side of caution by viewing all South Vietnamese civilians as potential enemies. Some American soldiers and units, uncertain as to who was an enemy and lost in the horror and confusion of war, responded by losing all sympathy for the South Vietnamese and in some cases intentionally attacking and abusing Vietnamese civilians. As a result of the "dirty" nature of the war, it was often impossible for observers to distinguish between true war crimes and atrocities on the one hand and horrible but "normal" wartime actions on the other.

The Nature of American and Vietnamese Atrocities

Kerrey's actions at Thanh Phong, although confusing and contentious, were not identified as a possible war crime until decades after the end of the war. Far more important for Americans struggling with the issue of war crimes in Vietnam were the atrocities that became known during the conflict. Nine months after that night at Thanh Phong, a U.S. Army platoon under the command of Lieutenant William L. Calley attacked the small Vietnamese village of My Lai, brutally raping women and slaughtering hundreds of unarmed, defenseless civilian men, women, and children. Several months after My Lai a Marine patrol entered the village of Son Thang and executed a number of civilians. Reports of the events at My Lai and Son Thang, along with numerous additional stories about atrocities perpetrated by American soldiers, enflamed passions in a United States already torn apart by debate about the Vietnam conflict. The My Lai massacre in particular became emblematic of the anger, shame, and confusion that Americans felt when discussing or debating Vietnam.

It is a mistake to believe that all or even most Americans in Vietnam committed war crimes or atrocities. The number and prevalence of such atrocities committed by Americans has probably been somewhat exaggerated, both by contemporary witnesses and by more recent popular culture portrayals of Vietnam-era soldiers, as in such films as *Full Metal*

Jacket and *Apocalypse Now.* This exaggerated view of the role war crimes played in the American war in Vietnam sprang from several sources, the most important of which was probably the antiwar movement. In using the issue of war crimes in Vietnam to try to discredit American intervention in Southeast Asia these critics were not always scrupulous about investigating the truth of the allegations they trumpeted. Several of the most serious war crimes allegations seized upon by the antiwar movement, such as those published in a controversial and influential 1970 book by Mark Lane entitled *Conversations with Americans*, ultimately proved false, casting doubt upon legitimate attempts to investigate atrocities. The mistaken impression that all American soldiers were committing war crimes and engaging in atrocities might also have arisen from more understandable and less nefarious sources as well. As historian Guenter Lewy argues in *America in Vietnam*, "While the Communists barred all observers except those known to be supportive of their cause, the war on the allied side took place in a fishbowl. Every mistake, failure, or wrongdoing was sooner or later exposed to view and was widely reported by generally critical press and television reporters."[7] In other words, because the media were interested in war crimes, which were sensational, journalists focused so much attention on reporting atrocities that Americans reading newspapers and watching television might have falsely concluded that war crimes in Vietnam were far more common than they actually were.

Violence, crime, and atrocity were by no means solely the province of the Americans; in fact, much of the horror of the war was perpetrated by the North Vietnamese and the Vietcong, who both routinely used torture, intimidation, and murder to fight for the creation of a Communist and unified Vietnam. While many of the atrocity stories told by American veterans may be exaggerated, it seems clear that the Vietcong engaged in an extensive campaign of assassination against South Vietnamese officials in order to terrorize the civilian population, and that they routinely tortured or executed South Vietnamese civilians who worked with or took assistance from American forces. As one U.S. Army lieutenant remembers, "[the North Vietnamese] would souvenir-hunt; take weapons, clothes, boots. And they would mutilate bodies."[8] The Vietcong also hid agents and weapons in civilian quarters and used the elderly, pregnant women, and children to attack U.S. forces or to carry bombs into American bases, thus further complicating American efforts to separate the enemy from the innocent. American servicemen in Southeast Asia were particularly terrified at the thought of being taken prisoner by the North Vietnamese. Such prisoners were often paraded publicly through villages and towns, where they were abused and spat upon by the local inhabitants and routinely beaten, tortured, and (according to some accounts) even killed.

National Policy

A third complicating factor in discussing and analyzing war crimes and atrocities in Vietnam is the fact that many of the "war crimes" that opponents of the war objected to, such as the deforestation of much of Vietnam with Agent Orange, the creation of free-fire zones, the bombing or destruction of seemingly civilian targets, and the invasion of and attacks on uninvolved countries such as Cambodia and Laos, were in fact essential elements of American strategy in Vietnam. That such strategies, though designed to "save" South Vietnam, could have negative or disastrous effects on civilian populations is best demonstrated by the comments of the off-quoted American major who reported on the razing of the village of Ben Tre during the 1968 Tet Offensive: "It became necessary to destroy it," he explained, "in order to save it."[9]

During the Vietnam conflict, as well as today, it is not always clear what actions constitute atrocities and what actions constitute legitimate military tactics. Shooting an unarmed woman holding a baby is murder, for instance—unless the woman is an enemy spy, or is hiding a bomb, in which case the killing is justified. Destroying a village is an atrocity—unless that village is functioning as a guerrilla base, in which case the destruction is a necessary military action. Many critics of U.S. policies in Vietnam particularly attacked what they saw as the American assumption that high-tech warfare, including the use of defoliants and high-altitude bombing, did not constitute war crimes. These critics echoed Daniel Ellsberg, the former military analyst who leaked the Pentagon Papers. Ellsberg wrote that "it would be shocking and perverse to condemn only rape and murder in wartime while continuing to tolerate the strategic bombing of noncombatants."[10] Supporters of U.S. actions in Vietnam countered by pointing out that the United States was not behaving all that differently from other nations, and that war itself brings death and destruction. As Lewy suggests, "This is not to say that allied military tactics in Vietnam were beyond reproach. However, a situation gradually developed in which the Americans and South Vietnamese could hardly do anything right."[11]

Even those critics of the war who felt that many American military actions constituted war crimes had difficulty deciding whether to blame American politicians and military leaders, who were responsible for what these critics saw as criminal policies, or American military personnel, who (under orders) were responsible for carrying out these policies on the tactical level. Those who defend whatever Bob Kerrey might have done in Thanh Phong, for instance—whether it was accidentally killing a number of civilians while firing at Vietcong or shooting prisoners to assist his team in withdrawing safely—have a point when they argue that Kerrey's actions were in line with official American policy. At the time of this mission, Kerrey's SEAL team had been operating for several weeks in the "Than Phu Secret Zone," a section of Vietnam that U.S. and South Vietnamese forces had designated a free-fire zone. This meant that American military personnel, including naval gunners offshore, bomber pilots overhead, and soldiers on the ground, were free to attack on sight any targets of opportunity—or anything they suspected was a target of opportunity. The Vietnamese in the free-fire zone were encouraged to move to "strategic hamlets," which South Vietnamese and American forces tried to protect; those who chose not to move were often regarded as Vietcong sympathizers or even Vietcong insurgents themselves. "In a free-fire zone we had permission to do it [kill whomever you wanted]," Kerrey told *Time* magazine in 2001. "And we had very aggressive instructions from our commanding officer in 1969 for how to deal with people there. And anybody that wasn't aware that this was going on, in my view, is lying."[12] If Kerrey's actions constitute a war crime, it remains unclear whether Kerrey or the military officials who came up with the concept of free-fire zones bears ultimate responsibility for the killings.

A Highly Politicized Issue

While the notion and definition of war crimes remain somewhat confused, and while debate continues over the distinction between atrocities and legitimate military tactics, the fact is that both American and Vietnamese forces committed war crimes and perpetrated atrocities during the Vietnam conflict. While the use of powerful flesh-burning weapons such as napalm or white phosphorus, or the use of defoliants such as Agent Orange—or, more controversially, the use of terror tactics to cow military forces or complicit civilian populations—is debatably justified by the military circumstances, it seems clear that there is no legitimate justification or excuse for the rape or murder of civilians, the torture of prisoners of war, the execution of political prisoners, or the mutilation of enemy corpses. The difficulty lies not in determining whether war crimes and atrocities were committed, but rather in determining exactly what happened and who was responsible.

It seems likely that the prevalence, extent, and exact nature of the atrocities and war crimes of the Vietnam period will remain unclear, partly because of the confused nature of the conflict and partly because the Vietnam War remains a potent political question today. When questions arose about Bob Kerrey's actions at Thanh Phong, for instance, Kerrey resigned and took up a position as the head of the New School University in New York. That questions about Vietnam-era atrocities retain enormous power in American politics was made even clearer during the 2004 presidential election. During that election, the Democratic nominee was Massachusetts senator John Kerry, who had once argued as a leader of Vietnam Veterans Against the War that U.S. forces were routinely perpetrating atrocities against the people of South Vietnam. Kerry's opponents created a controversial organization called "Swift Boat Veterans for Truth" and released a book (*Unfit for Command: Swift Boat Veterans Speak Out Against John Kerry*) in which they claimed that Kerry himself was guilty of committing war crimes. One veteran was quoted in the book as saying, "I will tell you in all candor that the only baby killer I knew in Vietnam was John F. Kerry."[13] While these comments by themselves probably did not cost Kerry the election, they effectively deterred him from using his record as a war hero to attack President George W. Bush.

"To know and understand what [Bob] Kerrey's Raiders did that night in Thanh Phong can be cathartic," argued journalists Johanna McGeary and Karen Tumulty in 2001.

"To condemn it is something else, requiring a clarity that was almost never available to young men shooting in the dark. It is a clarity our nation likewise never had at the time."[14] McGeary and Tumulty's point is well taken: it is important to face and struggle with questions of how American and Vietnamese forces conducted themselves during the Vietnam War. Unfortunately, the Vietnam conflict, which was enormously confused and complicated at the time, has become so politicized today that observers wishing to understand exactly what happened face a difficult task.

Notes

1. Quoted in Gregory L. Vistica, "What Happened in Thanh Phong," *New York Times*, April 29, 2001.
2. Mark Shields, *NewsHour with Jim Lehrer*, April 27, 2001.
3. Bob Kerrey, Associated Press, April 28, 2001.
4. Jonathan Schell, "War and Accountability," *Nation*, May 21, 2001.
5. Article 147, "Convention (IV) Relative to the Protection of Civilian Persons in Time of War," signed at Geneva, August 12, 1949.
6. Myra MacPherson, *Long Time Passing: Vietnam and the Haunted Generation.* New York: Doubleday, 1984, p. 489.
7. Guenter Lewy, *America in Vietnam.* Oxford, England: Oxford University Press, 1978, p. 223.
8. James Lawrence, quoted in MacPherson, *Long Time Passing*, p. 487.
9. Unnamed U.S. Army major, quoted in Peter Arnett, Associated Press report from Ben Tre, South Vietnam, February 7, 1968.
10. Quoted in MacPherson, *Long Time Passing*, p. 490.
11. Lewy, *America in Vietnam*, p. 223.
12. Quoted in Johanna McGeary and Karen Tumulty, "The Fog of War," *Time*, May 7, 2001.
13. Quoted in John E. O'Neill and Jerome R. Corsi, *Unfit for Command: Swift Boat Veterans Speak Out Against John Kerry.* Washington, DC: Regnery, 2004, p. 51.
14. McGeary and Tumulty, "The Fog of War."

Chapter 1

American War Crimes in Vietnam

1

American Soldiers Committed Atrocities in Vietnam

Myra MacPherson

Historians may never know how many American soldiers committed war crimes in Vietnam, what crimes those soldiers committed, and what happened to the victims. Even as the Vietnam conflict recedes into history, controversy continues over how many atrocity stories should be believed. In this excerpt from *Long Time Passing: Vietnam and the Haunted Generation*, Myra MacPherson describes talking to Vietnam veterans who claimed to be guilty of atrocities. It is clear, she explains, that the great majority of U.S. soldiers did not participate in atrocities, and even that some of the veterans who talked about committing atrocities were making up stories. MacPherson is nonetheless struck by the fact that almost every veteran she spoke with claimed to have known at least one "wild soldier." MacPherson concludes that while the country will never know the whole truth about what happened in Vietnam, and while some veterans are lying about being involved in atrocities, it seems certain that individual American soldiers did commit war crimes. Some of these soldiers, she adds, will forever be haunted by the memories of what they did in Southeast Asia.

MacPherson was for many years a celebrated writer for the *Washington Post* and has also written for the *New York Times* and other national publications. She is the author of several books and was nominated for a Pulitzer prize for *Long Time Passing: Vietnam and the Haunted Generation.*

Myra MacPherson, *Long Time Passing: Vietnam and the Haunted Generation.* New York: Doubleday, 1984. Copyright © 1984 by Doubleday, a division of Random House, Inc. Reproduced by permission of the author.

"What did my daddy do? Hell, he warn't nothin' but a whore-hoppin' drunk." Kenny sprawls on the chair, cowboy boots crossed. A USA belt buckle digs a furrow in his flabby belly; a Cat tractor hat is slung low on his brow. Red-tinged hair covers his arms, matching his beard. He looks past—not at—anyone. Kenny is doped beyond the beyond on the good grass he has cultivated in his lone garden in Alabama country wilderness.

He tells hard stories. Hard stories to listen to, undiluted in his fuzzy haze of drugs. He is a Southern kid who never had anything. Whose life, for good or bad, began and ended in Vietnam.

"Killin' goddamn gooks. That's the ultimate goal I ever achieved. When they put me in Vietnam, they got a damn zero to start with."

Kenny tells his story of atrocities and seems borderline crazy. It is disturbing, after all these months of being in sympathy with veterans, of liking so many of them, to meet someone who fits a "killer" stereotype. Kenny for years has sought relief through drugs and counseling—relief from the awful knowledge that he took pleasure in killing.

"I was a head man," Kenny drawls. "Cut a man's head off with an ax. It's not an easy task. I cut off twenty-one heads. We sold 'em to doctors and sech as that. They'd let 'em decay and have an actual skull they could use. . . ."

Anything Could Have Happened

Atrocity stories are staples of all wars, a blend of fact and fable, legendary embellishments and folklore. Vietnam's guerrilla war—fought in the midst of civilians and in deep jungles where booby-trapped deaths left soldiers aching for revenge—created its own special brutalities, rules and ethics.

One former intelligence officer, skeptical of some of the stories, finally shrugged and said, "It's really hard to separate what happened from what didn't. Anything *could* have happened there."

Some would have you believe that My Lai was commonplace. Others vehemently contend that most of the stories are concoctions of those who never saw combat.

Vietnam critics produced a first in war: American soldiers recanting in front of war-crimes tribunals [including the Vietnam Veterans Against the War's "Winter Soldier" investigation and British Lord Bertrand Russell's unofficial international tribunal]. For many Americans, no matter their revulsion to the war, there was something galling about Englishmen and Frenchmen (such as Bertrand Russell and Jean-Paul Sartre) calling tribunals to denounce America's role in Vietnam, given their countries' age-old record of brutal colonization. Sartre, for example, never suggested that France be brought before such a tribunal during *its* Vietnam War. Lord Bertrand Russell was, to be sure, a pacifist, but U.S. black writer James Baldwin—in general, a supporter of the war-crimes debate—wrote, "It might be considered more logical for any European, and especially any Englishman, to bring before an international tribunal the government of South Africa or the government of Rhodesia."

Atrocity stories are staples of all wars, a blend of fact and fable, legendary embellishments and folklore.

Still, worldwide outcry over our presence in Vietnam underscored the fact that no matter what we could have won militarily, a large portion of the world would see no political or moral victory. And it underscored the differences about Vietnam once again—why the sense of censure pervaded many veterans. For some participants, the war-crimes tribunal brought cleansing identity. Others, caught up as media "war-crimes heroes," testified far beyond their personal knowledge. "We found one guy who would have had to have been in nine places at the same time for his stories to be true," said one veteran who participated in the tribunal.

Truth or Lies?

No one could listen to Larry Mitchell and not be engrossed. He was a lieutenant in the Special Forces, he said. In 1982 Mitchell told me how he would sneak into camps and slit people's throats, including that of a young female Viet Cong sympathizer. Mitchell was captured, beaten, tortured; his ankles were shackled and bent so he could not sit or stand. One day following an escape attempt, his captors told him and another prisoner that they were going to be executed. "I and an Air Force colonel had to dig these graves. Then they bound our hands and the executioner stood behind us and I heard the click of the gun. I heard the shot. I was still alive. The colonel was not. They walked over and shot him again. They made me cover the grave. They didn't shoot me, for some reason."

The main reason was that none of it seems to have happened. Mitchell, as a member of Vietnam Veterans of America (VVA), was interviewed by national news magazines and television reporters; spoke at national Vietnam seminars. When a member of the MIA-POW became curious and checked the lists, Mitchell was not on any. The VVA confronted Mitchell—who had shown them a Xerox of discharge papers—and demanded that he verify his POW record and other stories. Mitchell never showed up again. "Believe me, we are a lot more careful now," said Rick Weidman of VVA. "We demand their Army record and keep it on file. It has a chilling effect on bullshit war stories." Mitchell is probably just one of countless hundreds who feel a sick need to exaggerate their role in the war. In their own way they demonstrate some need to belong to the most cataclysmic event of their time.

After a while, both stories call for suspension of belief. Could there really be that many pregnant women shot, that many gonads-in-the-mouth executions?

Kenny, therefore, is naturally viewed with suspicion, although the Vietnam veteran therapist who works with him feels his story is true. Kenny says he was in Vietnam during Tet 1968 on reconnaissance missions, roaming the jungles with small packs of soldiers.

He starts to tell in graphic detail of lifting an ax heavy with blood, after cutting off a man's head. "*That* affects me, lady.

"It was just a wild, mayhem thing. We had a guy in our outfit, Davis. Didn't smoke, didn't curse, didn't go after the whores. A guy you had to respect because he had so much will power." Kenny's head is low on his chest. "Davis kicked open a door of this old French building and was cut in two. When he was found, they had cut his head off and put it at his feet. And they had his penis in his mouth. The boys come back and said, 'Oh hell, Davis is a f—kin' *mess.*' The platoon sergeant, it really freaked him out. He just started screamin', 'Let's track 'em *down.*' We knew then he meant to kill anything—men, women, children, goddamn dogs, water buffalo. So we found 'em and killed 'em. I said to the sergeant, 'Bobo, what do we do now?' Tears was rollin' down. 'I want their goddamn heads,' he said. 'Just like they did to Davis. People in this area will *know* who we were when we get through.'"

I sigh. Another gonads-in-the-mouth story. Did *all* best buddies die that way? It is a legendary ultimate atrocity, described frequently, no matter when or where you were or how much action you saw. That and the pregnant woman shot in village firefights. When it came time for the body count, you turned over this body and discovered it was not only a woman, but a pregnant one. So you counted the baby.

After a while, both stories call for suspension of belief. Could there *really* be that many pregnant women shot, that many gonads-in-the-mouth executions? Yet they made the rounds of Vietnam then and in the States now. One reason for this is that they exemplify the two extremes of war's inhumanity. All those buddies mangled and mutilated, often booby-trapped after death by the VC, are distilled into the gonads-in-the-mouth atrocity. True certainly in some cases, apocryphal in others; a barbarous act made so commonplace in the telling that it could justify murderous mayhem as retribution. On the other hand, the pregnant woman "twofer" body count is usually told with revulsion for the U.S. government body-count obsession. "We" and "they." Committing atrocities together. . . .

The Viet Cong Committed Crimes Too

With Vietnam, the elitist opinion and later the mass opinion came to be that we were the aggressors, at worst, or that we were mired in a hopeless war, at best. Therefore the brutality was *perceived* differently; we were visiting atrocities upon innocent peasants. In the field, the gray reality was that some of those "innocent peasants" *were* the enemy. Children were not to be trusted. One Army doctor recalls pumping the stomachs of two GIs who bought beer from Vietnamese urchins. The "beer" was battery-acid fluid. Children set booby traps and led the enemy to their position. A 1968 Associated Press report tells of the North Vietnamese using children and women as shields in at least one battle—with Americans losing lives because they resisted shooting at them. Veterans often tell their own stories of individual civilian attacks. Trained to kill the enemy, it was not long before they were indiscriminately responding. And in such an uncensored war, Americans at home witnessed much of it. Atrocities on the other side, however, were often difficult to uncover and report.

James Lawrence, a lieutenant who saw fierce fighting against the NVA [North Vietnamese Army] regulars, says, "It really used to gall me when Jane Fonda went on about the horrible things Americans were doing after seeing some of the things the North Vietnamese did. They would souvenir-hunt; take weapons, clothes, boots. And they would mutilate bodies. The men who went back after the battle found Sergeant J—. (I would prefer you not use his name; I don't know if his family knew about this.) But they found him hung in a tree by his ankles and skinned, like you would a deer. Maybe they'd never seen a black before. I just don't know. We identified him by his gold teeth."

The ultimate North Vietnamese atrocity that we know of was the mass killing of hundreds at Hue during the Tet Offensive of 1968. Ours was My Lai. . . .

Everyone Knew One Wild Soldier

It is grossly unfair to tar the majority of Vietnamese veterans with the brush of My Lai. Most were not wanton or even wittingly accidental killers of civilians. Yet I am struck by the individual accounts of the disregard for human life that recur in interviews. Every combat veteran seems to remember at least one wild soldier.

Johnny, a former Green Beret: "We were goin' down this narrow road, and an MP beeped the jeep horn and bumped a motorcycle off, and these Vietnamese on it fell down. The third time he hit two young kids who worked on the military base. One of 'em died. I can still see his head hit the side of the jeep. The MP told me if I'm questioned to say he was only going thirty miles an hour and lost control. I told what I saw, but I don't know if anything happened to him. He was a career soldier."

Eddie, from South Boston: "War makes you *accept* violence. After one buddy was killed, a guy was torching a hootch when an old woman pleaded with him to stop. In a fit of madness, he set her on fire. Back home, he tried to commit suicide. He's dead already. He died that day in Vietnam."

Tom Vallely, now a member of the Massachusetts legislature: "I saw maybe three or four incidents of people going crazy, but My Lai was an aberration. It could never happen in my unit. They would have shot Calley. One guy shot up a villager after his friend was killed by a booby trap. Everyone grabbed him and kept him from shooting more."

It is grossly unfair to tar the majority of Vietnamese veterans with the brush of My Lai. . . . [Yet] every combat veteran seems to remember at least one wild soldier.

Others remember atrocities on the other side. A white Army infantry sergeant from Atlanta: "Two five-year-old boys were killed because they had associated with our units. While we were there, they gave us a lot of information, and one night a Viet Cong or NVA woman came into the village and killed both of them." A white marine from Westchester: "The ARVN [Army of the Republic of Vietnam, the South Vietnamese army] brought in a woman whose husband was a Viet Cong. They stripped her to the waist and took a generator . . . and they took one wire and put it to her left breast, the other to her right, and started to crank it . . ." Another veteran reported Viet Cong treatment of Americans. "They didn't believe in taking prisoners . . . They tortured our men, cut them up, and hung them in trees." A Los Angeles veteran: "They [VC sympathizers] were selling Zippo lighters, and the second time you would strike it, it would blow up in your hand . . ." And once again, back to our side—a Brooklyn Army veteran: "The back door of our vehicle was grated, and hot air from the engine comes out and that back deck gets to be 600 degrees after a while. It will burn through your shoes. That is where we would put our prisoners. Rope them, tie them, just throw them down there like a piece of cattle."

There were rapes and pot shots at buffalo with people riding on them, the indiscriminate blitz of helicopter fire and tossed grenades. Ears were being taken as souvenirs to such an extent that [General William C. Westmoreland, the

American commander in Vietnam] was forced to issue a directive denouncing the practice.

On the other hand, there were countless individual acts of moral courage. Men like Marine Colonel Michael Yunck, who refused to call an air strike on an enemy village filled with women and children. Instead, he took his helicopter low to pinpoint VC positions and got his leg shot off by a VC machine gun for his compassion. . . .

Collecting Gruesome Treasures

On February 10, 1970, Norman Ryman, Jr., mailed a package home to himself from Vietnam. It contained one photo album, one mirror, one pair of rubber sandals, two tiger fatigue shirts, one hat, one camouflage ascot, one brown shirt, one fatigue jacket, four pairs of tropical combat trousers, three tropical combat coats. And three human ears. Ryman, in a sworn statement, explained that two of the ears he took from a dead NVA soldier he had killed. "I then kept the ears as souvenirs. I got the third ear from a soldier that was assigned to the 101st Airborne. I paid five dollars for the ear. He had a large jar of ears that he was selling. He was a white guy with a mustache. I haven't seen him since."

Ryman's photo album contained pictures of mutilated "gooks."

Ryman was not alone in his practice of collecting ears. As Michael Herr wrote in *Dispatches:*

> There was a reedy little man in the circle who grinned all the time but hardly spoke. He pulled a thick plastic bag out of his pack and handed it over to me. It was full of what looked like large pieces of dried fruit. I was stoned and hungry, I almost put my hand in there but it had a bad weight to it. The other men were giving each other looks, some amused, some embarrassed and even angry. Someone had told me once, there were a lot more ears than heads in Vietnam; just information. When I handed it back he was still grinning, but he looked sadder than a monkey.

In a letter to all commanders in October 1967, Westmoreland called the practice of cutting ears and fingers from the bodies of dead enemies "subhuman." Some crackdowns in the souvenir hunting led to soldiers being court-martialed. Some, like Kenny, cut off the heads of corpses;

evidence was gained when soldiers posed for photo remembrances with the dead.

---

*For many among that small percentage of the
total combat force who committed atrocities,
there is little rest.*

Norman Ryman was in the States on leave when the package arrived. He was returning for his third tour of Vietnam, he loved it so. Although court-martialed, his case was mysteriously dismissed due to "lack of a speedy trial." Within days he was out of the Army by reason of a hardship discharge under honorable conditions. My Lai was on every news show, in all the front pages; Ryman's ear collecting would no doubt be a minor embarrassment. Ryman would later charge that he was rushed out of the Army and onto the streets in a psychotic state and should have been detained for treatment. . . .

It's Important to Remember

Some may question the point of rehashing the worst of the war at this distance. It is important to speak of it at some length because atrocities and acts of unnecessary violence remain one of the unspoken, awful legacies. Time muted the outrage. As there was more understanding of the kind of war young men had been asked to fight, Americans experienced yet another ambivalence—abhorrence for the acts, mingled with tolerance for the conditions of guerrilla warfare. The denial of collective national involvement must also be addressed. Atrocities are inevitable in wars, but Vietnam's frustrating war fought against civilians merely heightened that inevitability. If nothing else, this should be understood and examined as a caution for possible similar involvements in the future. Some people still argue the callous and inaccurate concept that "Orientals think very little of life." Because it has not come to grips with the kind of war we fought in Vietnam, America continues to hold a mixed bag of remembrances and confusion.

As for veterans who either participated in or witnessed acts of unnecessary violence, the *Legacies of Vietnam* study indicates a lingering trauma. Veterans remain deeply troubled. The study at first theorized that combat itself caused delayed stress. After reexamining the data, new analysis placed far greater emphasis on acts of unnecessary violence and atrocities as a major cause. The helplessness of being unable to control their environment in a guerrilla war "significantly contributed to the prevalence of abusive violence," often stemming from "rage, fear, and/or anxiety." The sample included 226 whites, 100 blacks, and 24 chicanos. About 29 percent of black vets were exposed to abusive violence and 32 percent whites; 14 percent of black vets actually participated in these acts and 8 percent of white vets. Yet they responded in different ways. Whites and blacks were equally troubled by exposure to abusive violence—in other words by events that they *witnessed*. Blacks were much more greatly troubled if they participated, feeling in retrospect that they had committed crimes against another racial group. Said a black infantryman from Chicago, "I raped a [Vietnamese] girl one time and prayed. God forgive me for doing that because I knew I was losing my mind." Whites who committed such acts remained, surprisingly, less stressed—as compared with those who only witnessed abusive violence. *Legacies* experts surmised that they belonged to a group who not only thought war was right, but had an abiding hatred for Vietnamese. They "denied the traumatic quality of their experience. Instead they numbed themselves to the toll of human misery they encountered," the study concluded. They subscribed to the "mere gook syndrome" and were more revenge-filled over the death of close buddies. One quote summed up this view: "Killing a gook was nothing really. I could have butchered them like nothing really. I had no feelings."

Yet, for many among that small percentage of the total combat force who committed atrocities, there is little rest. For Kenny, the "head man" of Alabama, . . . for those who participated in lesser My Lais, for the marine who recalls a time "when we were like animals," . . . and for others who keep their dark secrets close, they remember and remain haunted.

2

American Policy Makers Are Responsible for War Crimes in Vietnam

John F. Kerry

After graduating from Yale University in 1966, John F. Kerry served as a lieutenant in the U.S. Navy in Vietnam, where he was awarded numerous decorations, including a Silver Star, a Bronze Star, and three Purple Hearts. Kerry returned from Vietnam and became heavily involved with the Vietnam Veterans Against the War (VVAW), and in April 1971 he famously testified on behalf of the organization before the Senate Foreign Relations Committee. In this excerpt from that testimony, Kerry argues that American soldiers were unable to avoid committing war crimes because atrocities were a necessary and inevitable result of the ways in which the Vietnam conflict was being fought. The responsibility for those atrocities, Kerry concluded, lay not with the soldiers who committed the crimes, but rather with the generals and politicians who had ordered American troops into Southeast Asia and who had designed the policies and weapons of an unjust and mistaken war.

After the war, Kerry attended law school, then served as lieutenant governor of Massachusetts. In 1984 he was elected to the U.S. Senate. Senator Kerry received the Democratic presidential nomination in 2004, but ultimately lost the election to President George W. Bush. During the campaign, in which Kerry called upon his record as a war hero to support his bid for the presidency, a pro-Republican interest group called "Swift Boat Veterans for Truth" mounted a controversial campaign to discredit Kerry. The group claimed Kerry himself was a war criminal and that Kerry's support for the

John F. Kerry, testimony before the U.S. Senate Committee on Foreign Relations, Washington, DC, April 22, 1971.

VVAW had caused harm to American veterans and Americans held as prisoners of war in Vietnam. Kerry continues to serve in the U.S. Senate.

Mr. Kerry: I would like to say for the record, and also for the men behind me who are also wearing the uniforms and their medals, that my sitting here is really symbolic. I am not here as John Kerry. I am here as one member of the group of veterans in this country, and were it possible for all of them to sit at this table they would be here and have the same kind of testimony. . . .

The Winter Soldier Investigation

I would like to talk, representing all those veterans, and say that several months ago in Detroit, we had an investigation at which over 150 honorably discharged and many very highly decorated veterans testified to war crimes committed in Southeast Asia, not isolated incidents but crimes committed on a day-to-day basis with the full awareness of officers at all levels of command.

It is impossible to describe to you exactly what did happen in Detroit, the emotions in the room, the feelings of the men who were reliving their experiences in Vietnam, but they did. They relived the absolute horror of what this country, in a sense, made them do.

They told the stories at times they had personally raped, cut off ears, cut off heads, taped wires from portable telephones to human genitals and turned up the power, cut off limbs, blown up bodies, randomly shot at civilians, razed villages in fashion reminiscent of Genghis Khan, shot cattle and dogs for fun, poisoned food stocks, and generally ravaged the countryside of South Vietnam in addition to the normal ravage of war, and the normal and very particular ravaging which is done by the applied bombing power of this country.

We call this investigation the "Winter Soldier Investigation." The term "Winter Soldier" is a play on words of Thomas Paine in 1776 when he spoke of the Sunshine Patriot and summertime soldiers who deserted at Valley Forge because the going was rough.

We who have come here to Washington have come here

because we feel we have to be winter soldiers now. We could come back to this country; we could be quiet; we could hold our silence; we could not tell what went on in Vietnam, but we feel because of what threatens this country, the fact that the crimes threaten it, no reds, and not redcoats but the crimes which we are committing that threaten it, that we have to speak out.

Feelings of Men Coming Back from Vietnam

I would like to talk to you a little bit about what the result is of the feelings these men carry with them after coming back from Vietnam. The country doesn't know it yet, but it has created a monster, a monster in the form of millions of men who have been taught to deal and to trade in violence, and who are given the chance to die for the biggest nothing in history; men who have returned with a sense of anger and a sense of betrayal which no one has yet grasped.

As a veteran and one who feels this anger, I would like to talk about it. We are angry because we feel we have been used in the worst fashion by the administration of this country.

In 1970 at West Point, Vice President [Spiro T.] Agnew said "some glamorize the criminal misfits of society while our best men die in Asian rice paddies to preserve the freedom which most of those misfits abuse" and this was used as a rallying point for our effort in Vietnam.

We are angry because we feel we have been used in the worst fashion by the administration of this country.

But for us, as boys in Asia, whom the country was supposed to support, his statement is a terrible distortion from which we can only draw a very deep sense of revulsion. Hence the anger of some of the men who are here in Washington today. It is a distortion because we in no way consider ourselves the best men of this country, because those he calls misfits were standing up for us in a way that nobody else in this country dared to, because so many who have died would have returned to this country to join the misfits in their efforts to ask for an immediate withdrawal from South Vietnam, because so many of those best men have returned as quadriplegics and amputees, and they lie forgotten in Veterans' Administration hospitals in this country which fly the flag which so many have chosen as their own personal symbol. And we can not consider ourselves America's best men when we are ashamed of and hated what we were called on to do in Southeast Asia.

In our opinion, and from our experience, there is nothing in South Vietnam, nothing which could happen that realistically threatens the United States of America. And to attempt to justify the loss of one American life in Vietnam, Cambodia or Laos by linking such loss to the preservation of freedom, which those misfits supposedly abuse, is to us the height of criminal hypocrisy, and it is that kind of hypocrisy which we feel has torn this country apart.

We are probably much more angry than that and I don't want to go into the foreign policy aspects because I am outclassed here. I know that all of you talk about every possible alternative of getting out of Vietnam. We understand that. We know you have considered the seriousness of the aspects to the utmost level and I am not going to try to dwell on that, but I want to relate to you the feeling that many of the men who have returned to this country express because we are probably angriest about all that we were told about Vietnam and about the mystical war against communism.

What Was Learned in Vietnam

We found that not only was it a civil war, an effort by a people who had for years been seeking their liberation from any colonial influence whatsoever, but also we found that the Vietnamese whom we had enthusiastically molded after our own image were hard put to take up the fight against the threat we were supposedly saving them from.

We found most people didn't even know the difference between communism and democracy. They only wanted to work in rice paddies without helicopters strafing them and bombs with napalm burning their villages and tearing their country apart. They wanted everything to do with the war, particularly with this foreign presence of the United States of America, to leave them alone in peace, and they practiced the art of survival by siding with whichever military force was present at a particular time, be it Vietcong, North Vietnamese, or American.

We found also that all too often American men were dying in those rice paddies for want of support from their allies. We saw firsthand how money from American taxes was used for a corrupt dictatorial regime. We saw that many people in this country had a one-sided idea of who was kept free by our flag, as blacks provided the highest percentage of casualties. We saw Vietnam ravaged equally by American bombs as well as by search and destroy missions, as well as by Vietcong terrorism, and yet we listened while this country tried to blame all of the havoc on the Vietcong.

We rationalized destroying villages in order to save them. We saw America lose her sense of morality as she accepted very coolly a My Lai and refused to give up the image of American soldiers who hand out chocolate bars and chewing gum.

We learned the meaning of free fire zones, shooting anything that moves, and we watched while America placed a cheapness on the lives of Orientals.

We watched the U.S. falsification of body counts, in fact the glorification of body counts. We listened while month after month we were told the back of the enemy was about to break. We fought using weapons against "oriental human beings," with quotation marks around that. We fought using weapons against those people which I do not believe this country would dream of using were we fighting in the European theater or let us say a non-third-world people theater, and so we watched while men charged up hills because a general said that hill has to be taken, and after losing one platoon or two platoons they marched away to leave the hill for the reoccupation by the North Vietnamese because we watched pride allow the most unimportant of battles to be blown into extravaganzas, because we couldn't lose, and we couldn't retreat, and because it didn't matter how many American bodies were lost to prove that point. And so there were Hamburger Hills and Khe Sanhs and Hill 881's and Fire Base 6's and so many others.

Dying for a Mistake

Now we are told that the men who fought there must watch quietly while American lives are lost so that we can exercise the incredible arrogance of Vietnamizing the Vietnamese....

Each day to facilitate the process by which the United States washes her hands of Vietnam someone has to give up his life so that the United States doesn't have to admit something that the entire world already knows, so that we can't say that we have made a mistake. Someone has to die so that President Nixon won't be, and these are his words, "the first President to lose a war."

We are asking Americans to think about that because how do you ask a man to be the last man to die in Vietnam? How do you ask a man to be the last man to die for a mistake? But we are trying to do that, and we are doing it with thousands of rationalizations, and if you read carefully the President's last speech to the people of this country, you can see that he says, and says clearly: But the issue, gentlemen, the issue is communism, and the question is whether or not we will leave that country to the communists or whether or not we will try to give it hope to be a free people.

But the point is they are not a free people now under us. They are not a free people, and we cannot fight communism all over the world, and I think we should have learned that lesson by now. . . .

Lack of Moral Indignation in United States

Suddenly we are faced with a very sickening situation in this country, because there is no moral indignation and, if there is, it comes from people who are almost exhausted by their past indignations, and I know that many of them are sitting in front of me. The country seems to have lain down and shrugged off something as serious as Laos. . . .[1]

We rationalized destroying villages in order to save them. We saw America lose her sense of morality as she accepted very coolly a My Lai.

But we are here as veterans to say we think we are in the midst of the greatest disaster of all times now because they are still dying over there, and not just Americans, Vietnamese, and we are rationalizing leaving that country so that those people can go on killing each other for years to come.

1. The United States was engaged in a secret war in Laos while it was fighting the Vietnam conflict. The Vietcong and North Vietnamese were using a supply route known as the "Ho Chi Minh Trail," which ran through Laos. The United States and the South Vietnamese Army (ARVN) launched a massive (and unsuccessful) offensive in February of 1971 in order to cut this route. The offensive resulted in thousands of casualties.

Americans seem to have accepted the idea that the war is winding down, at least for Americans, and they have also allowed the bodies which were once used by a President for statistics to prove that we were winning that war, to be used as evidence against a man who followed orders and who interpreted those orders no differently than hundreds of other men in Vietnam.

You have to separate guilt from responsibility, and I think clearly the responsibility for what has happened there lies . . . with the men who designed free fire zones.

We veterans can only look with amazement on the fact that this country has been unable to see there is absolutely no difference between ground troops and a helicopter crew, and yet people have accepted a differentiation fed them by the administration.

No ground troops are in Laos, so it is all right to kill Laotians by remote control. But believe me, the helicopter crews fill the same body bags and they wreak the same kind of damage on the Vietnamese and Laotian countryside as anybody else, and the President is talking about allowing that to go on for many years to come. One can only ask if we will really be satisfied only when the troops march into Hanoi. . . .

The Extent of the Problem

We are here in Washington also to say that the problem of this war is not just a question of war and diplomacy. It is part and parcel of everything that we are trying as human beings to communicate to people in this country, the question of racism, which is rampant in the military, and so many other questions also, the use of weapons, the hypocrisy in our taking umbrage in the Geneva Conventions and using that as justification for a continuation of this war, when we are more guilty than any other body of violations of those Geneva Conventions, in the use of free fire zones, harassment interdiction fire, search and destroy missions, the bombings, the torture of prisoners, the killing of prisoners, accepted policy by many units in South Vietnam. That is what we are trying to say. It is party and parcel of everything.

An American Indian friend of mine who lives in the Indian Nation al Alcataz put it to me very succinctly. He told me how as a boy on an Indian reservation he had watched television and he used to cheer the cowboys when they came in and shot the Indians, and then suddenly one day he stopped in Vietnam and he said, "My God, I am doing to these people the very same thing that was done to my people." And he stopped. And that is what we are trying to say, that we think this thing has to end. . . .

The Responsibility for My Lai

Senator [Claiborne] Pell [addressing the Senate]: As the witness knows, I have a very high personal regard for him and hope before his life ends he will be a colleague of ours in this body. . . .

Finally, in connection with Lieutenant [William] Calley [commander of U.S. troops at My Lai], which is a very emotional issue in this country, I was struck by your passing reference to that incident.

Wouldn't you agree with me though that what he did in herding old men, women and children into a trench and then shooting them was a little bit beyond the perimeter of even what has been going on in this war and that that action should be discouraged. There are other actions not that extreme that have gone on and have been permitted. If we had not taken action or cognizance of it, it would have been even worse. It would have indicated we encouraged this kind of action.

Those Who Gave the Orders Are Guilty

Mr. Kerry: My feeling, Senator, on Lieutenant Calley is what he did quite obviously was a horrible, horrible, horrible thing and I have no bone to pick with the fact that he was prosecuted. But I think that in this question you have to separate guilt from responsibility, and I think clearly the responsibility for what has happened there lies elsewhere.

I think it lies with the men who designed free fire zones. I think it lies with the men who encourage body counts. I think it lies in large part with this country, which allows a young child before he reaches the age of 14 to see 12,500 deaths on television, which glorifies the John Wayne syndrome, which puts out fighting man comic books on the stands, which allows us in training to do calisthenics to four counts, on the fourth count of which we stand up and shout "kill" in unison, which has posters in barracks in this country with a crucified Vietnamese, blood on him, and underneath it says "kill the gook," and I think that clearly the responsibility for all of this is what has produced this horrible aberration.

Now, I think if you are going to try Lieutenant Calley then you must at the same time, if this country is going to demand respect for the law, you must at the same time try all those other people who have responsibility, and any aversion that we may have to the verdict as veterans is not to say that Calley should be freed, not to say that he is innocent, but to say that you can't just take him alone, and that would be my response to that.

Senator Pell: I agree with you. The guilt is shared by many, many, many of us, including the leaders of the get-out-now school. But in this regard if we had not tried him, I think we would be much more criticized and should be criticized. . . . By the same token I would hope the quality of mercy would be exercised in this regard for a young man who was not equipped for the job and ran amuck. But I think public opinion should think this through. We who have taken this position find ourselves very much in the minority.

Mr. Kerry: I understand that, Senator, but I think it is a very difficult thing for the public to think through faced with the facts. The fact that 18 other people indicted for the very same crime were freed and the fact among those were general and colonels. I mean this simply is not justice. That is all. It is just not justice.

3

American Tactics in Vietnam Were Justified and Legal

Guenter Lewy

In 1967 Bertrand Russell, an influential British academic and left-wing activist, organized an unofficial but prestigious "International War Crimes Tribunal" in Stockholm in order to hear claims that the United States was engaged in a criminal war in Southeast Asia. Ultimately, the Russell Tribunal concluded that many standard American military tactics were criminal. Among the tactics the tribunal condemned were the bombardment of targets such as villages and dams and the use of weapons such as napalm. In this excerpt from *America in Vietnam*, historian Guenter Lewy argues that while these standard American military policies and tactics were unpleasant, they were effective, were probably justified by the circumstances of the conflict, and (perhaps because international law is so complicated and ambiguous) were simply not illegal.

Lewy concludes that although it is clear that in isolated circumstances (such as at My Lai) Americans did commit atrocities, the United States' record in Vietnam does not support claims that Americans were waging a criminal war. Those who mistakenly concluded that the United States was waging such a criminal war, he adds, did so because they had distorted understandings of the war, were ignorant of actual American policies and practices, and were influenced by the massive and misleading propaganda campaigns of the Vietnamese Communists. Guenter Lewy is professor emeritus of political science at the University of Massachusetts, Amherst, and is the author of numerous books and articles.

E very war causes large-scale death and suffering, to the soldiers fighting it as well as to the civilian population on whose territory it is fought. But the moral outrages inherent in war are often ignored when the fighting is crowned with success and when the moral justification of the conflict is seen as sufficiently strong. Thus, despite the fact that the Allies in World War II engaged in terror-bombing of the enemy's civilian population and generally paid only minimal attention to the prevention of civilian casualties—even during the liberation of Italy and France—hardly anyone on the Allied side objected to these tactics. The war against nazism and fascism was regarded as a moral crusade in which the Allies could do no wrong, and the fact that it ended in victory further vindicated the use of means that were questionable on both legal and moral grounds.

The Vietnam war, on the other hand, dragged on for years without a real decision and was never perceived as a clear-cut struggle between good and evil. Moreover, while the Communists barred all observers except those known to be supportive of their cause, the war on the allied side took place in a fishbowl. Every mistake, failure or wrongdoing was sooner or later exposed to view and was widely reported by generally critical press and television reporters.

This is not to say that allied military tactics in Vietnam were beyond reproach. However, a situation gradually developed in which the Americans . . . could do hardly anything right.

This is not to say that allied military tactics in Vietnam were beyond reproach. However, a situation gradually developed in which the Americans and South Vietnamese could do hardly anything right. The Communists made skillful use of their worldwide propaganda apparatus to disseminate charges of American war crimes and they found many Western intellectuals only too willing to accept every conceivable allegation of wrongdoing at face value. Repeated unceasingly, these accusations eventually came to be widely believed. Among rational people, maintained Noam Chomsky, it was not in dispute that the "United States command is responsible for major crimes in the layman's sense of this term." "The fact is," declared the Committee of Concerned Asian Scholars, "that U.S. war crimes are an accepted and regularly used method of waging war in Indochina."

International Law Is Unclear

There soon emerged a veritable industry publicizing alleged war crimes. American servicemen stepped forward with articles and books dealing with their experience in Vietnam and became star witnesses before self-styled war crimes tribunals. Some of these proceedings concentrated on atrocities allegedly committed by individual soldiers or officers. . . . Others, like the International War Crimes Tribunal organized by Bertrand Russell, dealt with American military tactics like the creation of free-fire zones, the use of herbicides, fragmentation bombs, napalm, riot gas and the like.

The Russell tribunal, in large measure, relied on evidence supplied by VC/NVA [Vietcong/North Vietnamese Army] sources or collected in North Vietnam by persons closely aligned politically with the communist camp; the imprecision and slanted nature of these reports was obvious to most. As against the propagandistic information emanating from Hanoi, more careful observers of the Vietnam war acknowledged that legal judgment was made arduous because of the difficulty of establishing the facts about the conduct of allied military operations. Today the factual record is generally clear. On the other hand, the application of the law of war to battlefield practices remains a thorny task because many of the relevant provisions and rules are vague, were created for very different weapons in a very different world, and therefore are open to different interpretations. Hence acts branded as unlawful by the war crimes publicists are acts which, on a different reading of the law of war, can be considered perfectly legal.

The international law of war, aiming at mitigating the ravages of war, consists first of all of international treaties such as the Hague and Geneva conventions, binding the states which have ratified these treaties, and secondly of customary rules which are considered binding on all states, the proviso being that these rules coincide with general and regular practice on the part of the great majority of states. In addition, tactics or weapons may be deemed forbidden if they violate certain general principles of the law of war such as military necessity, humanity and chivalry. Finally, some lawyers invoke the so-called Martens clause, first appearing in Hague Convention IV of 1907 and named for the international lawyer George Frederick de Martens, as an additional law-creating source. This clause, included in the four Geneva conventions of 1949, lays down that states have obligations they are "bound to fulfill by virtue of the principles of the law of nations, as they result from the usages established among civilized nations, from the laws of humanity and the dictates of the public conscience." Yet if it is sometimes difficult to establish the correct application of certain clauses of treaty law or to ascertain the constancy of practice required for the binding character of customary law, these difficulties are magnified manifold in regard to the basic principles of the law of war. In particular, to derive specific prohibitions from "the laws of humanity and the dictates of the public conscience" becomes rather hazardous and can easily lead to confusing the law as it is and what it might or should be.

Vietnam's Legal Status Was Debatable

The legal situation in Vietnam was further complicated by the fact that international treaties like the Geneva conventions for the protection of the wounded, prisoners of war and the civilian population are treaties between states that have ratified these conventions and are applicable only to armed international conflicts between two or more of the contracting parties. The U.S. as well as South and North Vietnam had ratified the Geneva conventions; the U.S. and the GVN [Government of Vietnam (South Vietnam)] stated as early as 1965 that they regarded the hostilities an international conflict to which the Geneva conventions applied in full. However, many of the problematic tactics in Vietnam involved relations between the U.S. and GVN on one side and the VC and the civilian population of South Vietnam on the other, and here the various provisions of the Geneva conventions, as we will see soon, frequently were just not applicable. Even Article 3, common to all four conventions and designed to lay down certain minimal humanitarian principles to be observed in conflicts not of an international character, does not really fit the special conditions of modern insurgency warfare in which, for example, the distinction between "members of the armed forces" and "persons taking no active part in the hostilities" is distinctly hazy.

The question of whether a certain action was or was not justified by military necessity must be decided in terms of the way a commander judged the specific circumstances . . . at the time.

North Vietnam argued that the war was an internal domestic dispute and not an international conflict and denied that any of its armed forces were present in the South. The VC, for their part, announced that they did not regard themselves bound to international treaties to which the other belligerents subscribed though they promised to follow a humane and charitable policy toward prisoners who fell into their hands. Needless to say, all this created a host of legal ambiguities in this "international civil war" which greatly complicated the resolution of various rival claims. In this kind of situation, it will serve the cause of intellectual honesty to admit that the issues are indeed far from simple and that disagreements are possible on account of legal intricacies and not because some men are moral and others insensitive or corrupt. . . .

Bombardment and Destruction of Populated Areas

It is incontrovertible that the allied military effort in Vietnam was characterized by the lavish use of firepower and caused much destruction of property and a large number of civilian casualties. From this many critics of American policy in Vietnam have concluded that American combat practices violated the law of war and that the U.S. therefore was guilty of war crimes. U.S. battlefield tactics, charged Prof. Richard A. Falk in 1971, involved "the massive use of cruel tactics directed indiscriminately against the civilian population in flagrant violation of the minimum rules of war." [A group of] . . . American theologians [including Martin Luther King, Jr., Harvey G. Cox, Robert F. Drinan, and others] concluded: "When we measure American actions in Vietnam against the minimal standards of constraint established by the Hague Convention of 1907 and the Geneva Conventions of 1929 and 1949, our nation must be judged guilty of having broken almost every established agreement for standards of human decency in time of war."

An analysis of the applicable law of war suggests a somewhat different conclusion. It first should be recognized that the VC's practice . . . of converting hamlets into fortified strongholds was one of the main reasons for the occurrence of combat in populated areas. The existing law of war was not written to encompass this kind of warfare; to the extent that it does apply to insurgency warfare it prohibits such tactics, for it seeks to achieve maximum distinction between combatants and innocent civilians. Resistance fighters must carry arms openly and have "a fixed distinctive sign recognizable at a distance" [according to the Geneva Convention Relative to the Treatment of Prisoners of War]; the civilian population may not be used as a shield—"the presence of a protected person may not be used to render certain points or areas immune from military operations" [according to the Geneva Convention Relative to the Treatment of Civilian Persons in Time of War]. Whether the VC were justified in disregarding these internationally accepted legal norms, as some writers have argued, is a question to which I shall return. The fact remains that by carrying the war into the hamlets and by failing properly to identify their combatants, the VC exposed the civilian population to grave harm.

It is well established that once civilians act as support personnel they cease to be noncombatants and are subject to attack.

Hague Convention IV (1907) prohibits "the attack or bombardment, by whatever means, of towns, villages, dwellings, or buildings which are undefended." "Firing on localities which are undefended and without military significance," stated a 1966 MACV [Military Assistance Command, Vietnam (U.S. military headquarters)] directive, "is a war crime." However, according to the general practice of states, once a village or town is occupied by a military force or is fortified, it becomes a defended place and is subject to attack.

The same holds true for civilian homes used to store war materiel. Such places become legitimate military objectives and injuries suffered by the civilian population are considered incidental and unavoidable. Indeed, even hospitals lose their immunity if "they are used to commit, outside their humanitarian duties, acts harmful to the enemy" and due warning has been given to cease such use [according to the Geneva Convention]. One can question the wisdom of attacking the VC once they had holed up in a hamlet and regard such a response as counterproductive in a counterinsurgency setting, but the practice is surely not a violation of the law of war.

Particular Tactics Were Judgment Calls

Even when attacking a defended place, the rule of proportionality must be observed—"loss of life and damage to property must not be out of proportion to the military advantage to be gained" [according to the U.S. Department of the Army]. In the context of Vietnam, this meant, for example, that an American unit drawing a single sniper shot from a village was not justified in obliterating the entire village by using artillery and air strikes. But what if there are five snipers blocking an important bridge situated in a hamlet? How can a commander make a precise estimate of the size of the enemy unit which is firing upon his men? One sniper using an automatic weapon can sound like a platoon. These were the kinds of difficult situations faced by American officers in Vietnam who, as always in combat, had to act on incomplete information.

There is no question that some military men panicked and overreacted to provocation. But . . . the question of whether a certain action was or was not justified by military necessity must be decided in terms of the way a commander judged the specific circumstances of the situation at the time. "If the facts were such," declared the Nuremberg tribunal . . . "as would justify the action by the exercise of judgment, after giving consideration to all the factors and existing possibilities, even though the conclusion reached may have been faulty, it cannot be said to be criminal." If a commander in Vietnam employed artillery and air strikes against a village—whether because he overestimated the size of the enemy force faced or because he sought to avoid excessive casualties to his own men—and his action caused the loss of civilian life, he may have hurt the cause of pacification but his action probably was not illegal. Illegal conduct could arise if the commander was negligent—if he *could* or *should* have known that the use of overwhelming firepower was not really necessary to overcome enemy resistance—but the determination of such wrongdoing in a fluid battlefield situation is extremely difficult.

Not All Vietnamese Were Civilians

Another source of confusion in judging the matter of civilian casualties was the designation by many critics of all villagers as innocent civilians. We know that on occasion in Vietnam women and children placed mines and booby traps, and that villagers of all ages and sexes, willingly or under duress, served as porters, built fortifications, or engaged in other acts helping the communist armed forces. It is well established that once civilians act as support personnel they cease to be noncombatants and are subject to attack. Allied troops usually counted all dead persons found after battle in a defended hamlet as VC, and there existed, of course, no way in which they could have distinguished willing helpers of the VC from those pressed into service. They also could not tell who had been engaged in such support and who had been a mere innocent bystander caught in the battle. Here again we see the unfortunate consequence of the fact that the VC chose to fight from within villages and hamlets which provided useful cover, avenues of escape and a source of labor for the building of fortifications. Inevitably, the civilian population was involved in the fighting.

The American record in Vietnam with regard to observance of the law of war is not a succession of war crimes . . . as many critics of the American involvement have alleged.

The law of war forbids the destruction of personal property "except where such destruction is rendered absolutely necessary by military operations" [according to the Geneva Convention]. It does allow the destruction of fortifications. Since in Vietnam the VC often built their trenches, bunkers and escape tunnels right in the middle of hamlets—if not in, around and underneath huts and houses—the destruction of fortifications usually amounted to the destruction of homes or even entire hamlets. This is what happened in the widely publicized case of Cam Ne in 1965, as well as in numerous other instances, and critics soon started accusing U.S. forces of conducting a scorched-earth policy. In response to one such complaint, involving the burning of two villages in Binh Dinh province, the Army's assistant judge advocate general explained that "the two Vietnamese villages were not burned as a reprisal for the hostile fire that came from the houses in the village. They were destroyed because the houses and tunnel networks connecting them constituted enemy fortified positions." In actual practice it often was difficult to distinguish an enemy bunker, constructed right under a hut, from a shelter built by a villager for his protection, and there undoubtedly were many cases where houses were destroyed without compelling justification. . . .

The American Record Is Mixed

The American record in Vietnam with regard to observance of the law of war is not a succession of war crimes and does not support charges of a systematic and willful violation of existing agreements for standards of human decency in time of war, as many critics of the American involvement have alleged. Such charges were based on a distorted picture of the actual battlefield situation, on ignorance of existing rules of engagement, and on a tendency to construe every mistake of judgment as a wanton breach of the law of war. Further, many of these critics had only the most rudimentary understanding of international law and freely indulged in fanciful interpretations of conventions and treaties so as to make the American record look as bad as possible. Finally, there were the communist propagandists who unleashed a torrent of largely unsubstantiated charges with the hope that at least some of the lies would stick. This is indeed what happened.

If the American record is not one of gross illegality, neither has it been a model of observance of the law of war. Impeccable ROE [Rules of Engagement], based on applicable legal provisions, were issued, but their observance was often inadequate and the American command failed to take reasonable steps to make sure that they would be properly enforced. The greatly improved training courses in the law of war, which were started after the My Lai incident had revealed flagrant disregard of the ROE in some units, indicates what kinds of corrective action could and should have been taken years earlier. Moreover, practice often dictated policy. The use of RCA [riot control agents—tear gas], for example, escalated quickly beyond the original humanitarian purpose for which RCA had been originally authorized. Similarly, the employment of herbicides was begun on the basis of a legal memorandum prepared in 1945 for a very different situation, and this was symptomatic of the lack of adequate legal review of newly introduced weapons and tactics. In both cases, the U.S. was put on the defensive by the pressure of public opinion and eventually had to make adjustments in policy after the fact.

In October 1974 DOD [the Department of Defense] promulgated a new instruction which required the judge advocate general of each military service to conduct a legal review of all weapons in order to insure that their intended use in armed conflict was consistent with the obligations assumed by the U.S. under applicable international law, including both treaties to which the U.S. was a party and customary international law. The instruction also required that a legal review take place before a contract for the production or procurement of new weapons was awarded. Another directive, issued 5 November 1974, obligated the JCS [Joint Chiefs of Staff] to insure that "rules of engagement issued by unified and specified commands are in consonance with the law of war." Again, one may wish that such instructions had been issued in 1964 rather than in 1974.

There is no way of being certain that human suffering on the part of the civilian population of South Vietnam could have been mitigated by greater attention to legal considerations and by better enforcement of the ROE. Even if these rules had been applied more firmly, there can be little doubt that the American reliance on heavy weapons and the lavish use of firepower would have exacted a heavy toll in lives, injuries and the destruction of property. American commanders applied the motto "Expend Shells Not Men," and while fighting in often heavily populated areas this manner of warfare was bound to lead to heavy casualties among the civilian population. Failure to pursue an alternative strategy, which would have paid more attention to the proverbial "hearts and minds," is probably a contributory cause of the ultimate collapse of South Vietnam, but it cannot be considered a violation of the law of war.

4

Henry Kissinger's Policies Led to War Crimes

Christopher Hitchens

Some people insist that U.S. political and military leaders who set policies and gave orders that led to war crimes are as culpable, if not more so, than the soldiers who committed the individual acts. No case is more controversial than that of Henry Kissinger, the German-born Harvard political scientist who served as the U.S. national security adviser and secretary of state during the presidencies of Lyndon Johnson, Richard Nixon, and Gerald Ford. Kissinger heavily influenced U.S. policies around the world, acted as the go-between in the negotiations that opened relations between the United States and China, promoted U.S. support of anti-Communist regimes in Central and South America, and ultimately arranged a cease-fire with North Vietnam. (For arranging this cease-fire, Kissinger was awarded the Nobel Peace Prize in 1973.)

In this excerpt from his *Harper's* magazine article "The Case Against Henry Kissinger," Christopher Hitchens argues that Kissinger was a war criminal because his policies resulted in atrocities and implicated the United States in war crimes. Hitchens charges that Kissinger orchestrated bloody military actions in Vietnam in order to improve Richard Nixon's reelection chances, and waged aggressive war against civilian populations. He suggests that Kissinger should perhaps be tried for war crimes for these actions. Hitchens, a self-proclaimed "political gadfly," is a prolific author, journalist, and pundit who has written for or contributed to many publications, including the

Atlantic Monthly, Harper's, the *Wall Street Journal,* and the *Washington Post.*

It will become clear, and may as well be stated at the outset, that this is written by a political opponent of Henry Kissinger. Nonetheless, I have found myself continually amazed at how much hostile and discreditable material I have felt compelled to omit. I am concerned only with those Kissingerian offenses that might or should form the basis of a legal prosecution: for war crimes, for crimes against humanity, and for offenses against common or customary or international law, including conspiracy to commit murder, kidnap, and torture. . . .

The historical record of the Indochina war is voluminous, and the resulting controversy no less so. This does not, however, prevent the following of a consistent thread. Once the war had been unnaturally and undemocratically prolonged, more exorbitant methods were required to fight it and more fantastic excuses had to be fabricated to justify it. . . .

Kissinger Supported "Total War" Tactics

In December 1968, during the "transition" period between the Johnson and Nixon administrations, the United States military command turned to what General Creighton Abrams termed "total war" against the "infrastructure" of the Vietcong/National Liberation Front insurgency. The chief exhibit in this campaign was a six-month clearance of the province of Kien Hoa. The code name for the sweep was Operation "Speedy Express."

It might, in some realm of theory, be remotely conceivable that such tactics could be justified under the international laws and charters governing the sovereign rights of self-defense. But no nation capable of deploying the overwhelming and annihilating force described below would be likely to find itself on the defensive. And it would be least of all likely to find itself on the defensive on its own soil. So the Nixon-Kissinger Administration was not, except in one unusual sense, fighting for survival. The unusual sense in which its survival *was* at stake is set out, yet again, in the stark posthumous testimony of H.R. Haldeman [Richard Nixon's chief of staff]. From his roost at Nixon's side he describes a

Kissingerian moment on December 15, 1970:

> K[issinger] came in and the discussion covered some of
> the general thinking about Vietnam and the P's [Presi-
> dent's] big peace plan for next year, which K [Kissinger]
> later told me he does not favor. He thinks that any pull-
> out next year would be a serious mistake because the
> adverse reaction to it could set in well before the '72
> elections. He favors, instead, a continued winding
> down and then a pullout right at the fall of '72 so that
> if any bad results follow they will be too late to affect
> the election.

One could hardly wish for it to be more plainly put than
that. (And put, furthermore, by one of Nixon's chief parti-
sans with no wish to discredit the re-election.) . . .

Thus the colloquially titled "Christmas bombing" of
North Vietnam, continued after that election had been
won, must be counted as a war crime by any standard. The
bombing was not conducted for anything that could be de-
scribed as "military reasons" but for twofold political ones.
The first of these was domestic: a show of strength to ex-
tremists in Congress and a means of putting the Democratic
Party on the defensive. The second was to persuade South
Vietnamese leaders such as President [Nguyen Van]
Thieu—whose intransigence had been encouraged by
Kissinger in the first place—that their objections to Ameri-
can withdrawal were too nervous. . . .

When the unpreventable collapse occurred in Cambodia
and Vietnam, in April and May 1975, the cost was infinitely
higher than it would have been seven years previously. . . .

A U.S. General Hinted
Kissinger Should Be Executed

Some statements are too blunt for everyday, consensual dis-
course. In national "debate," it is the smoother pebbles that
are customarily gathered from the stream and used as pro-
jectiles. They leave less of a scar, even when they hit. Occa-
sionally, however, a single hard-edged remark will inflict a
deep and jagged wound, a gash so ugly that it must be cau-
terized at once. In January 1971 there was a considered
statement from General Telford Taylor, who had been chief
U.S. prosecuting counsel at the Nuremberg trials. Review-
ing the legal and moral basis of those hearings, and also the

Tokyo trials of Japanese war criminals and the Manila trial of Emperor Hirohito's chief militarist, General Yamashita Tomoyuki, Taylor said that if the standard of Nuremberg and Manila were applied evenly, and applied to the American statesmen and bureaucrats who designed the war in Vietnam, then "there would be a very strong possibility that they would come to the same end [Yamashita] did." It is not every day that a senior American soldier and jurist delivers the opinion that a large portion of his country's political class should probably be hooded and blindfolded and dropped through a trap-door on the end of a rope. . . .

Kissinger's Policies Led to the Deaths of Civilians

From a huge menu of possible examples, I have chosen cases that involve Kissinger directly and in which I have myself been able to interview surviving witnesses. The first, as foreshadowed above, is Operation "Speedy Express":

My friend and colleague Kevin Buckley, then a much admired correspondent and Saigon bureau chief for *Newsweek*, became interested in the "pacification" campaign that bore this breezy code name. Designed in the closing days of the Johnson-Humphrey Administration, it was put into full effect in the first six months of 1969, when Henry Kissinger had assumed much authority over the conduct of the war. The objective was the American disciplining, on behalf of the Thieu government, of the turbulent Mekong Delta province of Kien Hoa.

Thus the colloquially titled "Christmas bombing" of North Vietnam . . . must be counted as a war crime by any standard.

On January 22, 1968, [U.S. Secretary of Defense] Robert McNamara had told the Senate that "no regular North Vietnamese units" were deployed in the Delta, and no military intelligence documents have surfaced to undermine his claim, so that the cleansing of the area cannot be understood as part of the general argument about resisting Hanoi's unsleeping will to conquest. The announced purpose of the Ninth Division's sweep, indeed, was to redeem many thousands of villagers from political control by the National Liberation Front (NLF), or "Vietcong" (VC). As Buckley found, and as his magazine, *Newsweek*, partially disclosed at the rather late date of June 19, 1972,

> All the evidence I gathered pointed to a clear conclusion: a staggering number of noncombatant civilians—perhaps as many as 5,000 according to one official—were killed by U.S. firepower to "pacify" Kien Hoa. The death toll there made the My Lai massacre look trifling by comparison. . . .

> The Ninth Division put all it had into the operation. Eight thousand infantrymen scoured the heavily populated countryside, but contact with the elusive enemy was rare. Thus, in its pursuit of pacification the division relied heavily on its 50 artillery pieces, 50 helicopters (many armed with rockets and mini-guns) and the deadly support lent by the Air Force. There were 3,381 tactical air strikes by fighter bombers during "Speedy Express.". . .

> "Death is our business and business is good," was the slogan painted on one helicopter unit's quarters during the operation. And so it was. Cumulative statistics for "Speedy Express" show that 10,899 "enemy" were killed. In the month of March alone, "over 3,000 enemy troops were killed . . . which is the largest monthly total for any American division in the Vietnam War," said the division's official magazine. When asked to account for the enormous body counts, a division senior officer explained that helicopter gun crews often caught unarmed "enemy" in open fields. . . .

> There is overwhelming evidence that virtually all the Viet Cong were well armed. Simple civilians were, of course, not armed. And the enormous discrepancy between the body count [11,000] and the number of captured weapons [748] is hard to explain—except by the conclusion that many victims were unarmed innocent civilians. . . .

> The people who still live in pacified Kien Hoa all have vivid recollections of the devastation that American firepower brought to their lives in early 1969. Virtu-

ally every person to whom I spoke had suffered in some way. "There were 5,000 people in our village before 1969, but there were none in 1970," one village elder told me. "The Americans destroyed every house with artillery, air strikes, or by burning them down with cigarette lighters. About 100 people were killed by bombing, others were wounded and others became refugees. Many were children killed by concussion from the bombs which their small bodies could not withstand, even if they were hiding underground."

Other officials, including the village police chief, corroborated the man's testimony. I could not, of course, reach every village. But in each of the many places where I went, the testimony was the same: 100 killed here, 200 killed there.

Other notes by Buckley and his friend and collaborator Alex Shimkin (a worker for International Voluntary Services who was later killed in the war) discovered the same evidence in hospital statistics. In March 1969, the hospital at Ben Tre reported 343 patients injured by "friendly" fire and 25 by "the enemy," an astonishing statistic for a government facility to record in a guerrilla war in which suspected membership in the Vietcong could mean death. And Buckley's own citation for his magazine—of "perhaps as many as 5,000" deaths among civilians in this one sweep—is an almost deliberate understatement of what he was told by a United States official, who actually said that "*at least* 5,000" of the dead "were what we refer to as non-combatants"—a not too exacting distinction, as we have already seen, and as was by then well understood. [*Italics mine.*]

Americans Seemed to Target Civilians

Well understood that is to say, not just by those who opposed the war but by those who were conducting it. As one American official put it to Buckley,

"The actions of the Ninth Division in inflicting civilian casualties were worse [than My Lai]. The sum total of what the 9th did was overwhelming. In sum, the horror was worse than My Lai. But with the 9th, the civilian casualties came in dribbles and were pieced out over a long time. And most of them were inflicted from the air and at night. Also, they were sanctioned by the command's insistence on high body-counts. . . . The result was an inevitable outcome of the unit's command policy."

The earlier sweep that had mopped up My Lai—during Operation "Wheeler Wallawa"—had also at the time counted all corpses as those of enemy soldiers, including the civilian population of the village, who were casually included in the mind-bending overall total of 10,000.

Confronted with this evidence, Buckley and Shimkin abandoned a lazy and customary usage and replaced it, in a cable to *Newsweek* headquarters in New York, with a more telling and scrupulous one. The problem was not "indiscriminate use of firepower" but "charges of quite *discriminating* use—as a matter of policy in populated areas." Even the former allegation is a gross violation of the Geneva Convention; the second charge leads straight to the dock in Nuremberg or The Hague.

Since General Creighton Abrams publicly praised the Ninth Division for its work, and drew attention wherever and whenever he could to the tremendous success of Operation "Speedy Express," we can be sure that the political leadership in Washington was not unaware. Indeed, the degree of micromanagement revealed in Kissinger's memoirs quite forbids the idea that anything of importance took place without his knowledge or permission.

Kissinger Was Personally Involved in Making Decisions

Of nothing is this more true than his own individual involvement in the bombing and invasion of neutral Cambodia and Laos. Obsessed with the idea that Vietanamese intransigence could be traced to allies or resources external to Vietnam itself, or could be overcome by tactics of mass destruction, Kissinger at one point contemplated using thermonuclear weapons to obliterate the pass through which ran the railway link from North Vietnam to China, and at another stage considered bombing the dikes that prevented North Vietnam's irrigation system from flooding the country. Neither of these measures (reported respectively in Tad Szulc's history of Nixon-era diplomacy, *The Illusion of Peace*, and by Kissinger's former aide Roger Morris) was taken, which removes some potential war crimes from our bill of indictment but which also gives an indication of the regnant mentality. There remained Cambodia and Laos, which supposedly concealed or protected North Vietnamese supply lines.

As in the cases postulated by General Telford Taylor, there is the crime of aggressive war and then there is the question of war crimes. In the postwar period, or the period governed by the U.N. Charter and its related and incorporated conventions, the United States under Democratic and Republican administrations had denied even its closest allies the right to invade countries that allegedly gave shelter to their antagonists. . . .

The degree of micromanagement revealed in Kissinger's memoirs quite forbids the idea that anything of importance took place without his knowledge or permission.

All this law and precedent was to be thrown to the winds when Nixon and Kissinger decided to aggrandize the notion of "hot pursuit" across the borders of Laos and Cambodia. As William Shawcross reported in his 1979 book, *Sideshow*, even before the actual territorial invasion of Cambodia, for example, and very soon after the accession of Nixon and Kissinger to power, a program of heavy bombardment of the country was prepared and executed in secret. One might with some revulsion call it a "menu" of bombardment, since the code names for the raids were "Breakfast," "Lunch," "Snack," "Dinner," and "Dessert." The raids were flown by B-52 bombers, which, it is important to note, fly at an altitude too high to be observed from the ground and carry immense tonnages of high explosive; they give no warning of approach and are incapable of accuracy or discrimination. Between March 1969 and May 1970, 3,630 such raids were flown across the Cambodian frontier. The bombing campaign began as it was to go on—with full knowledge of its effect on civilians and flagrant deceit by Mr. Kissinger in this precise respect.

To wit, a memorandum prepared by the Joint Chiefs of Staff and sent to the Defense Department and the White House stated plainly that "some Cambodian casualties would be sustained in the operation" and that "the surprise effect of attack could tend to increase casualties." The target district for "Breakfast" (Base Area 353) was inhabited, explained the memo, by about 1,640 Cambodian civilians; "Lunch" (Base Area 609), by 198 of them; "Snack" (Base Area 351), by 383; "Dinner" (Base Area 352), by 770; and "Dessert" (Base Area 350), by about 120 Cambodian peasants. These oddly exact figures are enough in themselves to demonstrate that Kissinger must have been lying when he later told the Senate Foreign Relations Committee that areas of Cambodia selected for bombing were "unpopulated."

As a result of the expanded and intensified bombing campaigns, it has been officially estimated that as many as 350,000 civilians in Laos and 600,000 in Cambodia lost their lives. (These are not the highest estimates.) Figures for refugees are several multiples of that. In addition, the widespread use of toxic chemical defoliants created a massive health crisis that naturally fell most heavily on children, nursing mothers, the aged, and the already infirm. That crisis persists to this day.

Richard Nixon and Kissinger Share the Guilt

Although this appalling war, and its appalling consequences, can and should be taken as a moral and political crisis for American institutions, for at least five United States presidents and for American society, there is little difficulty in identifying individual responsibility during this, its most atrocious and indiscriminate stage. Richard Nixon, as commander in chief, bears ultimate responsibility and only narrowly escaped a congressional move to include his crimes and deceptions in Indochina in the articles of impeachment, the promulgation of which eventually compelled his resignation. But his deputy and closest adviser, Henry Kissinger, was sometimes forced, and sometimes forced himself, into a position of virtual co-presidency where Indochina was concerned. . . .

It is therefore impossible for him to claim that he was unaware of the consequences of the bombings of Cambodia and Laos; he knew more about them, and in more intimate detail, than any other individual. Nor was he imprisoned in a culture of obedience that gave him no alternative, or no rival arguments. Several senior members of his own staff, most notably Anthony Lake and Roger Morris, resigned over the invasion of Cambodia, and more than two hundred State Department employees signed a protest addressed to Secretary of State William Rogers. Indeed, both Rogers and Secretary of Defense Melvin Laird were opposed to the secret bombing policy, as Kissinger himself records with some disgust in his memoirs. Congress also was opposed to an extension of the bombing (once it had agreed to become informed of it), but even after the Nixon-Kissinger Administration had undertaken on Capitol Hill not to intensify the raids, there was a 21 percent increase of the bombing of Cambodia in the months of July and August 1973. The Air Force maps of the targeted areas show them to be, or to have been, densely populated.

The truly exorbitant death tolls all occurred on Henry Kissinger's watch; were known and understood by him; were concealed from Congress, the press, and the public by him.

Colonel [Ray] Sitton does recall, it must be admitted, that Kissinger requested the bombing avoid civilian casualties. His explicit motive in making this request was to avoid or forestall complaints from the governments of Prince Sihanouk. But this does no more in itself than demonstrate that Kissinger was aware of the possibility of civilian deaths. If he knew enough to know of their likelihood, and was director of the policy that inflicted them, and neither enforced any actual precautions nor reprimanded any violators, then the case against him is legally and morally complete. . . .

Kissinger Tried to Hide the Truth

One reason that the American command in Southeast Asia finally ceased employing the crude and horrific tally of "body count" was that, as in the relatively small but specific case of Operation "Speedy Express" cited above, the figures began to look ominous when they were counted up. Sometimes, totals of "enemy" dead would turn out, when computed, to be suspiciously larger than the number of claimed "enemy" in the field. Yet the war would somehow drag on, with new quantitative goals being set and enforced. Thus, according to the Pentagon, the following are the casualty figures between the first Lyndon Johnson bombing halt in March 1968 and February 26, 1972:

Americans: 31,205

South Vietnamese regulars: 86,101

"Enemy": 475,609

The U.S. Senate Subcommittee on Refugees estimated that in the same four-year period, rather more than 3 million civilians were killed, injured, or rendered homeless.

In the same four-year period, the United States dropped almost 4,500,000 tons of high explosive on Indochina. (The Pentagon's estimated total for the amount dropped in the entire Second World War is 2,044,000.) This total does not include massive sprayings of chemical defoliants and pesticides.

It is unclear how we count the murder or abduction of 35,708 Vietnamese civilians by the CIA's counterguerrilla "Phoenix program" during the first two and a half years of the Nixon-Kissinger Administration. There may be some "overlap." There is also some overlap with the actions of previous administrations in all cases. But the truly exorbitant death tolls all occurred on Henry Kissinger's watch; were known and understood by him; were concealed from Congress, the press, and the public by him; and were, when questioned, the subject of political and bureaucratic vendettas ordered by him.

Chapter **2**

The My Lai Massacre

1

The Americans Slaughtered Vietnamese at My Lai

The People's Army of Vietnam (PAVN)

On March 16, 1968, U.S. soldiers under the command of Lieutenant William Calley invaded the South Vietnamese hamlet of My Lai, which they suspected of harboring Vietcong insurgents. During the following several hours, Calley's soldiers rounded up and executed hundreds of residents of the village, most of whom were unarmed civilians. At least a few of the victims were tortured and raped. Although some soldiers reported what had happened (some soldiers had in fact saved Vietnamese civilians by facing down their fellow soldiers with weapons), news of the massacre remained sparse until almost a year after the incident, when an American soldier sent letters describing the event to his superiors and to various politicians.

The Vietcong and the North Vietnamese were aware of what had happened at My Lai and made efforts to publicize their version of the event throughout Vietnam and the world. This description of the My Lai massacre is excerpted from a translation of a document authored by the political section of a unit of the People's Army of Vietnam (PAVN), the North Vietnamese Army (NVA), and captured by the U.S. 1st Infantry Division (Airmobile) in December 1969. This document was clearly designed by the PAVN as propaganda and was probably intended to inflame the population of South Vietnam.

In this account of the massacre the PAVN paints a picture of a bucolic, peaceful, and productive village invaded by brutish, homicidal, bearded Americans. Interestingly, the PAVN authors did acknowledge that residents of the My Lai area had previ-

The People's Army of Vietnam, "PAVN Political Section Report on Massacre at My Lai," March 1968.

ously engaged in actions designed to "harass" American forces—thus supporting U.S. reports that My Lai gave shelter and support to the Vietcong. The PAVN authors go on to describe how American soldiers raped and executed numerous women, children, and elderly villagers and explain that when the survivors returned to My Lai to bury the dead they found that all of the bodies had been mutilated.

The massacre of 502 compatriots conducted by the US imperialists in Son My Village, Son Tinh District, Quang Ngai Province on 16 Mar[ch] [19]68.

Picturesque and prosperous Son My with firm spirited people.

Son My is a coastal village belonging to Son Tinh District, Quang Ngai Province. It includes My Lai and My Hoi Hamlets. The population there is about 700. The people earn their living by fishing, planting sugarcane, making sugar, and farming. The scenery is beautiful. Bamboo and coconut trees around the village shade the roads, and green willows grow throughout the four seasons. On the river, boats are anchored together snuggly. . . .

They [the people of My Lai] did not side with the US, but they could not have expected the tragedy that would befall them that day.

Since the day the US aggressors set foot on South Vietnamese soil to fulfill their aggressive schemes and were stationed in Quang Ngai, the people there often harassed them, causing them to eat and sleep uneasily. To undermine the fighting spirit of the Son Tinh people, the US aggressors drowned over 1,000 people living in An Hoa and An Bien Villages in the sea in May [19]69, and had previously massacred 502 innocent people in Son My (in Mar[ch] [19]68).

The Day of the Massacre

A grievous day. On 16 Mar[ch] [19]68, as in previous days, the daily activities of the people went on normally. The people got up early, cooked their meals and then went to work. In the village, children played under the shade of the trees. Women carrying their babies in their arms talked with one another about the coming harvest. Young girls helped their mothers to strike coconut fibers. In another hamlet, girls wove fish nets skillfully. Under the big trees, some young boys crowded around old men who were plaiting ropes for pulling boats. Here and there were heard the friendly crowing of roosters and buffaloes and cows moving. In the sound of the wind, there reverberated a melodious folk song. Some brown fishing boats appeared on the sea.

US soldiers, with thick bearded faces filled with anger, spread out to search the trenches in the village.

Six-thirty:
Suddenly, the deafening noise of guns was heard. Artillery fire was fiercely and indiscriminately conducted on the village from the US post at Nui Gam Mountain, Son Tinh Sub-Sector, and Quang Ngai Sector.

As usual, the people led their children to take shelter in trenches (possibly tunnels).

They did not side with the US, but they could not have expected the tragedy that would befall them that day.

The enemy conducted shellings incessantly for half an hour.

After the shelling, and on receiveing orders to "destroy Son My," the commanders of the 11th US Independent Brigade used 11 helicopters to strafe Son My, then they landed troops.

U.S. Troops Were Ordered to Kill

This US unit was Company C, 1st Battalion, 20th Regiment, 11th Independent Brigade, commanded by Captain Medine [*sic*—actually Captain Ernest Medina] and First Lieutenant Coly [*sic*—actually First Lieutenant William Calley]. The US soldiers rushed to the village without meeting any resistance and spread out to search the village and hamlets. In accordance with the drafted plan, the commanders ordered their soldiers to burn houses, cut trees, and kill cattle and people.

In a moment, 300 wooden and brick houses were turned

into flames, with smoke rising skyward. The US troops chopped down the trees and killed the cattle. The noise of guns, the crackle of burning bamboo, the noise of falling trees, and the cries of dogs, cats, buffalo, and cows created a terrible and fearful sound. A number of inhabitants who rushed to their houses to stamp out the fires were shot to death. Afterwards, the US troops were ordered to drive the people out of their trenches for annihilation.

US soldiers, with thick bearded faces filled with anger, spread out to search the trenches in the village. They pulled up eight of the 15 people hiding in Brother Le's trench and killed them with grenades. They then detonated a mine in the trench, destroying it and burying the remaining seven people. Sister Vo Thi Thu was sitting in her trench with Lien, a young girl, carrying her child. They pulled her out of the trench and fired at her. She could only tell Lien: "Please tell my husband that I hid the 6,000$ (SVN) (118$ SVN=$1.00 US) at the foot of the coconut tree."

The most heartbreaking fact was that all the dead bodies were badly mangled. The villagers buried these dead bodies together in one mass grave.

She fell down, still carrying her child who was suckling at the mother's breasts. An American rushed to her, pointed at the child and shouted "Viet Cong, Viet Cong" (?). He then pulled and threw burning thatch all over the mother and child. Another American threw some more thatch to make the flame rise higher. In the afternoon, the (local) compatriots dug through the ashes and saw that the child had been burned to ashes and just two black lips were left on the mother's breasts. Mrs Mui and Mrs Min each had two children. They were hiding in a trench and the US troops exploded a mine to kill all of them. Mrs Trinh was having a meal with her children. The US troops rushed into (her house) and fired at her two children. Mr Duc was forced to leave the trench he was hiding in and was shot in the head. The blind grandmother of Miss Lien was killed as soon as she left the trench. Miss Lien cried: "Grandfather; Grandmother has been killed." As soon as she cried, the US troops caught her grandfather and set fire to his beard and killed him. Mrs Thi was killed by the US troops. Mrs Mao, 72 years old, was thrown into a fire. Miss Lien's aunt was killed while she was hiding in a trench. Miss Minh was killed. Her body remained against the wall of a trench, her face looked so indignant. Mrs Ngon was eight months pregnant; she was raped until she had a miscarriage and then was killed. Mrs Vo Thi Mai, who had just given birth to a baby 10 hours before, was also raped to death. Mrs Dam, 60 years old, was raped and stabbed in the stomach. Miss Mui, 14 years old, was hung up on a tree and raped. After that, she was thrown into a fire. Old man Truong Pho, (number missing) years old had his beard cut, was thrown into a well, and then the US troops threw a grenade into the well to kill him. Mrs Lien, who had two children, was killed. She only had enough time to give a last recommendation to her mother, "Please look after your grandchildren." Then she died.

Mopping Up the Witnesses

When all the people were forced to leave the trenches (possibly tunnels), they were gathered at the ditch close to Mr Nhieu's house and slaughtered (by the troops, using) M-16 rifles, M-60 machine guns, grenades and M-79 grenade launchers.

Those who were not killed outright were stabbed to death with bayonets. The dead bodies were piled on top of one another five-high.

Blood, brains, bones and flesh lay in the water and sand, and were hardly recognizable. Many children were not hit with bullets, but suffocated in puddles of blood. Sister Di's child, eight months old, a survivor, was found in a puddle of blood.

Piles of dead bodies were left in disorder in ponds, in corners of vegetable gardens, in houses, in stables, on floors, in front of gates, in kitchens and in ditches. For five hours after the massacre of the Son My villagers, the Americans stayed there to find and kill any survivors. They did not withdraw until late in the afternoon. Survivors, covered by dead bodies, crawled from the piles of dead bodies, their bodies stained with blood. In the evening, (Son My) villagers came back to bury their relatives. The most heartbreaking fact was that all the dead bodies were badly mangled. The villagers buried these dead bodies together in one mass grave.

2

The Attack on My Lai Was Justified and Effective

Ta Linh Vien

In defense of the actions of U.S. troops at My Lai, some Americans argued that the village was a hotbed of Vietcong (VC) activity. By sheltering VC fighters and working for the VC themselves, the residents of the village had transformed themselves from civilians into combatants. South Vietnamese officials, who were familiar with the terrorist tactics of the Vietcong and the North Vietnamese, similarly regarded the action at My Lai as justified, and some were even confused at the furious reaction in the United States to the news of the massacre.

The following excerpt is 1970 testimony to military lawyers involved in the case of Lieutenant William Calley, the U.S. commander at My Lai. Ta Linh Vien, a former South Vietnamese official, explains through an interpreter that he had long known that My Lai was a "combat village" inhabited by Communist agents and sympathizers. Vien also states that he was one of the officials who requested that U.S. forces attack My Lai and concludes that Vietcong activity in the area was enormously reduced for years after the American action around My Lai. In Vien's view, the My Lai massacre was a necessary and successful step in the war against the Communist enemy. According to his testimony, Vien was at one point the adjutant chief of the Census Grievance Center, and so was effectively working for the Central Intelligence Agency. ("Census Grievance" was a covert CIA operation designed to place

Ta Linh Vien, testimony to the U.S. Military, Quang Ngai City, Republic of Vietnam, December 8, 1970.

agents in South Vietnamese villages and was linked to the covert CIA assassination program in South Vietnam.)

━━━━━━━━━━━━━━━━━━━━━━━━━━━━━━━━━━

Cpt Eckhardt [Captain William Eckhardt, Chief Prosecutor]: Let the record reflect that the time is now 1420 hours. This conference is convened at Kramer Compound, Quang Ngai City, Republic of Vietnam. The purpose of this hearing is to obtain a sworn statement of Mr. Ta Linh Vien. Present at this conference are Mr. Vien, Sergeant Tan, Specialist Bull. Sergeant Tan is the interpreter, and Specialist Bull is the reporter. Also present are Captain Eckhardt, representing the government; Captain Heintz, Gowing, Lanham, Arkow and Link, representing the following accused: Sergeant Torres, Specialist T'Souvas, Private Hutson and Private Smith.

[*Mr. Ta Linh Vien* was sworn and testified as follows:]
Questions by Captain Eckhardt:
Q: What is your full name, please, sir?
A: Ta Linh Vien.
Q: Where do you live?
A: Du Xanh, D-u X-a-n-h, Village, Dung Xia, D-u-n-g X-i-a, District, Quang Ngai Province.
Q: What is your occupation, please, sir?
A: Right now I no occupation at all. . . .
Questions by Captain Lanham:
Q: Mr. Vien, what was your duty in March of 1968? . . .
A: I would like to ask him about the date.
Q: What did he just tell you?

I Was an Intelligence Chief in Quang Ngai

A: He said that he was the Adjutant Chief of Census Grievance Center.[1]
Q: Is that all he said?
A: And also take care of intelligence.
Q: Intelligence?
A: Yes, sir.
Q: For what section of Vietnam—what section of Vietnam did you work in?

---

1. Census Grievance (CG) was a CIA covert action program designed to obtain information on the Vietcong by using agents stationed in villages or operating as part of armed propaganda teams.

A: Adjutant Chief of Census Grievance Center, and also take care of the intelligence for the whole Quang Ngai Province.

Q: When did you begin your duties as the Assistant Chief of the Census Grievance Center?

A: I perform my duties in March of 1969.

Q: Since March of 1969?

A: 1969.

Q: What did you do before March of 1969?

A: Before that I also member of Grievance—Census Grievance Center, but I was not Adjutant. I just a take care of situation section.

Q: That's what section?

A: Situation section.

Q: Situation section. How long had you done that?

A: Until first of March, 1970.

All of the people living in My Lai, women, children, the old man, old woman, everybody . . . have some weapon at home.

Q: How long had you been working with the Census Grievance Center before you became Assistant Chief?

A: He say he started to work with this Center since the Center established until this organization not operated any more.

Q: When was the Center established?

A: 20 September 1965.

Q: So you have worked with the Census Grievance Center since 20 September 1965 up through 19—at least March of 1969 when you became Assistant Chief, is that correct?

A: Yes, sir.

Q: How many people worked for you there?

A: He said the whole Province. He have more than 300 cadre. In the office there are only 11 personnel.

Q: Did these cadre live in the hamlets and villages throughout Quang Ngai Province?

A: Yes. All cadre living in the Quang Ngai Province. He said this Center regroup all of them the people working with Center.

Q: Do they live only in government hamlets or did some live in Communist controlled hamlets?

A: We have a officer cadre everyday working with the people right in the government controlled areas, and we also have some secret agent. They have enough legal paper to go to the Communist controlled area and to go to government controlled area, and besides that we have some special agent living right in VC controlled area.

Q: Did these cadre report to you?

A: Yes, sir.

Q: From these cadre, did you gain a knowledge of VC activity in Quang Ngai Province?

A: When we still perform the duty, we always follow up the situation every day. We not only take care of our enemy situation, but we also take care of our friendly situation.

Q: From these cadre, did you gain a knowledge as to which villages and hamlets were loyal to the government, and which villages and hamlets were loyal to the Communists?

A: Yes. We follow the situation on the map every day, and US Embassy personnel all the way come to check the situation every day.

My Lai Was an Enemy Stronghold

Q: From what these cadre told you, did you consider that the village of My Lai was a VC stronghold?

A: He say, yes, all of the eastern area of Son Tinh—you know, is completely controlled by VC along with the roads and all of villages in eastern sector of Son Tinh; My Lai is one of the hamlets in—under VC control.

Q: Do any VC live in My Lai? Did any VC live in My Lai before March of 1968?

A: Yes. Before March of 1968, VC were in My Lai Hamlet. He said not only VC in My Lai Hamlet, but VC also in Son My Village. In Son My Village their district agency—VC district agency in Son My Hamlet—Son My Village.

Q: In—from you knowledge of Communist activities in Quang Ngai Province, would you say that women and children often assist the VC?

A: Yes. He say women, children—even children, small, also used by VC to detonate mine.

Q: From your knowledge of Communist activities in Quang Ngai Province, would you say that the area around and in My Lai was heavily mined and booby-trapped?

A: Yes. He said many booby-trap and mine around My Lai, and some cadre—some of his cadre were hit by mine in that area, and he would always try to protect—try his best to protect the wounded and bring back to the hospital. He said he would like to say more.

---

*My Lai is one hamlet providing security by VC.
. . . Whenever US troops or ARVN come to that
hamlet. . . they fire against US troops and
ARVN.*

Q: Please do.

A: He said My Lai—nearly everybody—you know, My Lai is a combat village, and many ARVN get killed in My Lai—around My Lai, and all of the people living in My Lai, women, children, the old man, old woman, everybody—you know, have some weapon at home. Everytime all of family took over there, they use all of men to go against friendly units. In case if somebody get lost in that area, the people do get killed.

Q: Let the record indicate that the witness made some diagrams on the floor. Could you, please, explain what he was talking about when he made diagrams on the floor?

A: He said My Lai is one hamlet providing security by VC—you know. They build fence around hamlet, and they dig foxhole around the hamlet; they have fortification in that area. Whenever US troops or ARVN come to that hamlet—you know, they use—they fire against US troops and ARVN.

Q: In your discussion of My Lai, are you talking about it before March of 1968?

A: Yes, before March of 1968. . . .

The People in My Lai Were Warned to Leave

Q: Did you hear of an operation the Americans conducted in My Lai during March of 1968?

A: Yes, I know that situation. I have a secret agent in Son My Village, and every day they report to me all of situation happen in Son My Village. Sometime they report of operation of allied and ARVN forces in that area.

Q: What was your understanding of what took place

when the Americans went into My Lai during March of 1968? Tell us what he has told you so far.

Cpt Eckhardt: Let him, if he could, translate that much and then we'll pick up from there.

Questions by Captain Lanham:

Q: Tell us what he has told you so far.

A: Before US operation in My Lai, I know the government have some plan going to have a big operation in that area; they called saturation area operation. Before that helicopter all these broadcasts around that area—around that area, east of Son Tinh and east of Son Tinh, S-o-n T-i-n-h, District, and east of Binh Son, B-i-n-h S-o-n. I, myself already heard the broadcasts twice, and because helicopter—you know, flew around that area, and also flew around the city. The government controlled—told all of the people living in My Lai, Son Guan, Son Tinh area, they called all of the people in that area if anybody not support VC have to move out of that area and return to the government area, they will be assisted by the government or else if anybody still living in that area, the government have—will have a big operation in that area, and that area will be considered a—a free-fire zone; if anybody still living in that area will be get killed.

Q: Continue.

A: After that for awhile, I have a report from my cadre in that area, there is some ARVN operation in that area, and after that I cannot remember the date, but maybe on 16 March my cadre report to me there was a big US operation in that area, and US troop meet a hard time before breaking in that hamlet—My Lai Hamlet.

Q: Have you ever suggested to anyone that it would be helpful to the pacification of Quang Ngai Province if My Lai were destroyed?

A: I cannot catch.

I Suggested That My Lai Be Destroyed

Q: Did you ever suggest, ever ask anyone, ever tell anyone that it would assist in destroying the Communism to destroy My Lai?

A: He said after checking—collecting information, he ordered to have some suggestion to have a big operation around that area.

Q: Say that again. I didn't hear that.

A: After collecting some good information, I also—and inform all other agencies and suggested one operation to destroy Son My area, because we have information that in Son My their one district can prevent—prevent soldiers—agency in that area.

Q: How soon before the 16th of March, 1968, did you make this suggestion?

A: He say he recommended have operation to destroy all of structures in that area before 1968 new year.

Q: To which officials was this suggestion made?

A: He say I think my suggestion already carry out by allied troop and ARVN after allied troop and ARVN collecting some more information.

Q: Was this an official suggestion of the Census Grievance Committee?

A: He say he don't know what military authorities use his suggestion or not, but when US troop or ARVN have operation in that area, he think some how the plan something on his suggestion.

All Residents of My Lai Were Communist Agents

Q: When he said destroy the Son My and My Lai area, did he mean destroy structures, all people and all livestock?

A: Yes, if in a civilian in that area a good decision of the government they order to move out of that area and live under government controlled area. He think all of civilian in that area, all of them are VC sympathizer or they have some relative, son or daughter working for VC, as they try to stay in that area to live, they don't want to leave that area, so they consider all of them aides of the VC.

Q: You said that you had heard before March of 1968 that an operation was going to be conducted against My Lai, is this correct?

A: He said before March of 1968, I also know some operation in that area, but after US operation in My Lai area, I have received a report from cadre.

Q: Was it your understanding that the operation that was to be conducted at My Lai was to carry out your suggestion?

A: He said, I don't believe that they depend on our information. Our allied force have a big operation in that area. I think after allied force collect information from many intelligence agencies before they have big operation in that area, because the other information have the same information as I already got from my cadre.

All of the civilian in that area would be
considered as Communist.

Q: Which American agencies did the Census Grievance Center report to?
A: All of the classified are not so important information. We make report to province chief, and by the same time we also inform US Embassy in Quang Ngai, and all of the urgent information concerning about the situation—VC situation, we inform directly to all of US troops—US force of US agencies.
Q: US Agencies near us?
A: US forces—US force.
Q: US forces?
A: US forces.
Q: Which particular US force, do you recall?
A: He said, because in Son My, there are no US forces in that area, so he don't give information to that area, but some area—in Son My there are no US troops force in that area, so we not give information to any unit in Son My area, but in Duc Pho there are some US units, so at anytime we have good information, we give that information to some US unit in that area.
Q: Did you ever give information or report to the Americal Division?
A: He said he just sent report to embassy, and embassy have to take care of it.
Q: The embassy send the information to the correct American unit, is that true?
A: Yes, sir, that is true. All information sent to allied— embassy have to take care.
Q: Do you know whether any other intelligence sources besides the Census—the Grievance Center made similar recommendations as yours as to destroying My Lai?
A: He said, long time, I cannot remember, but I think one agency called the PRU, P-R-U—
Maj. Thong: P-R-U, PRU.
A: PRU. He said that information also—agency also

collects many information in that area, and sometime that agency exchange information to his agency.

Q: After March of 1968, did Communist activity around the Son My area decrease significantly, drop a lot?

A: Until—he said starting in April until now VC pressure around Son My Village disappear greatly deal until now.

Q: Did the Census—Did the Census Grievance Committee ever receive any complaints from inhabitants of My Lai or the nearby areas about the American operation in March of 1968?

A: No.

Q: Why not?

A: Because—because a civilian in that area is a Communist, so the hamlet don't have any at all to his Center.

Q: You said all civilians in that area are Communist?

A: All.

Cpt Eckhardt: Would you repeat the whole answer again, please?

Wit: He said all of the civilian in that area would be considered as Communist. If a civilian of the government—you know, any time they have an operation they move to government controlled area.

3

The Main Perpetrator at My Lai Became a National Hero

Michal R. Belknap

The American public did not become aware of what had happened in My Lai in March 1968 until November 1969, when independent journalist Seymour Hersh broke the story. Americans were instantly divided over the question of whether Lieutenant William Calley, who had commanded the troops at My Lai, had done anything wrong. In March 1971 Calley was found guilty of premeditated murder and was sentenced to life imprisonment; he was the only defendant convicted. Probably as a result of public pressure, Calley's sentence was soon reduced, and in 1974 his conviction was entirely overturned.

In this excerpt from *The Vietnam War on Trial*, historian Michal R. Belknap argues that although most people did not approve of what had happened at My Lai, many Americans supported Calley and opposed his conviction. Oddly, Belknap explains, some of these Americans supported Calley because they supported the war, while others supported Calley because they thought the war was immoral. The great majority, Belknap adds, suspected that Calley was being used as a scapegoat by the generals and politicians who were truly responsible for what had happened.

Michal R. Belknap is currently a professor of law at California Western School of Law and an adjunct professor of history at the University of California at San Diego. He is the author of several books, including *American Political Trials*.

Michal R. Belknap, *The Vietnam War on Trial: The My Lai Massacre and the Court-Martial of Lieutenant Calley*. Lawrence: University Press of Kansas, 2002.

"He's been crucified," screamed a woman outside the courthouse after Lieutenant Calley's sentence was announced. "He should get a medal," she added in disgust. Soon America's airwaves were alive with the sounds of "The Battle Hymn of Lieutenant Calley." After a voice-over about a little boy who wanted to grow up to serve his country, Nashville's Tony Nelson trolled:

> My name is William Calley, I'm a
>   soldier of this land,
> I've vowed to do my duty and to
>   gain the upper hand,
> But they've made me out a villain,
>   they have stamped me with a brand
> As we go marching on.

Within three days after the court-martial ended, the Plantation label sold over 200,000 copies of Nelson's improbable ode to a mass murderer. Three weeks later *Life* magazine observed, "The case of William Calley simply will not rub away. . . . [H]is name still crops up daily." Calley, a man a court-martial had convicted of killing twenty-two Vietnamese civilians, had become a national hero. Every measure of public opinion revealed popular outrage at his conviction. Members of Congress joined hundreds of thousands of Americans in protesting the verdict, and President Nixon intervened personally in the case. Although [prosecutor] Captain [Aubrey] Daniel challenged the propriety of his action, the people backed the president, for Calley was their hero. To them the little lieutenant was a victim of a war with which they had become disaffected and a government they did not trust.

Virtually everyone thought Calley had been made a scapegoat.

Senator Robert Taft Jr. (R. Ohio) recognized that "the widespread reaction against the Calley conviction was ill-informed and in error," but his was one of only a few dissenting voices. *The Nation* maintained that "there can be no quarrel with the verdict," and the *Washington Evening Star* found it "difficult to see how the six members of the Fort Benning jury could have found otherwise." *Commonweal* warned against "deadening our abhorrence of acts like My-lai." Likewise, the *Chicago Tribune*, while pointing out that the Vietcong had also committed savage war crimes, conceded, "Two wrongs, of course, don't make a right."

Politicians Overwhelmingly Supported Calley

While a few publications accepted the verdict, Taft's fellow politicians overwhelmingly condemned it. Governor George Wallace of Alabama, who had been the American Independent Party's presidential candidate in 1968 and was seeking the 1972 Democratic nomination, made freeing Calley a campaign theme. After asking Selective Service officials in his state to see if they could suspend the draft there, Wallace headed for Columbus to visit the lieutenant and take part in a rally that also featured Georgia's lieutenant governor, Lester Maddox. Maddox wrote to President Nixon, urging him "to immediately utilize the vast power of your office to free 1st Lt. William L. Calley, Jr." Not to be outdone, Governor Jimmy Carter of Georgia proclaimed "American Fighting Man's Day" and asked citizens to drive with their headlights turned on. Mississippi's governor, John Bell Williams, informed Vice President Spiro Agnew that his state was "about ready to secede from the union" over Calley. The Louisiana legislature and the Texas Senate passed resolutions urging Nixon to pardon the convicted killer, and the Arkansas Senate joined them in requesting executive clemency. In Florida the city commission of Plant City and the mayor and approximately 3,000 citizens of Crestview enlisted in the pro-Calley army. While support for Calley was strongest in the South, his backers included politicians from throughout the country. The elected officials of Artesia, New Mexico, protested the verdict, and that state's Representative Manuel Lujan Jr. urged the president to pardon Calley, or at least reduce his sentence. The Kansas House of Representatives and even the Guam legislature called for executive clemency. The county commissioners of Lancaster County, Pennsylvania, a New York assemblyman, and the mayor of Concord, California, all wrote to the president to complain about the verdict. In Pittsfield, Illinois, the entire draft board resigned "in protest of the results of the court-martial of Lt. William Calley, Jr."

Protesting politicians and public officials were only echoing the sentiments of their constituents. Polls revealed overwhelming opposition to the conviction and life sentence Calley had received. Louis Harris reported to the White House over the weekend after the court-martial ended that "a slight plurality of the American public [36 to 35 percent] disagree with the verdict of the military tribunal," and 29 percent "could not make up its mind on whether or not Lt. Calley should have been declared guilty or innocent." Indecision quickly evaporated, as did most of the support for the verdict. A telephone survey done for the president by the Opinion Research Center on 1 April found 78 percent of those interviewed disagreed with the conviction and life sentence imposed on Calley. On 7 April, the Gallup Poll reported that a special survey, commissioned by *Newsweek* had found that only 9 percent of Americans approved of the court-martial's finding that he was guilty of premeditated murder, while 79 percent disapproved. When a Wheeling, West Virginia, radio station asked its listeners to comment on the verdict, 1,412 of them responded; only 15 agreed with it. Even Harris's polling organization eventually found 65 percent disapproval of the guilty verdict, versus only 24 percent approval. Since most Americans thought Calley should have been acquitted, it was hardly surprising that 79 percent of those surveyed by Gallup considered life imprisonment too harsh a penalty. A poll done for the president found 51 percent of the public wanted Nixon to free Calley, and another 28 percent thought the chief executive should reduce his sentence. A mere 9 percent agreed with the court-martial that the former platoon leader ought to spend the rest of his life in prison.

Hundreds of Thousands of Americans Complained

Opposition to the conviction and sentence was intense as well as widespread. During the trial Calley's supporters had bombarded him with fan mail. By mid-February he had already received more than 10,000 letters, only 7 of which were derogatory. After the jury returned its verdict, a stream of fan mail turned into a torrent, reaching 10,000 pieces per day. To keep up with it, Calley's girlfriend and secretary had to buy an automatic letter opener. As late as 19 April, supportive missives were still pouring into his apartment at the rate of 2,000 per day. . . .

The hundreds of pieces of mail that poured into the

Court of Military Appeals would have been barely noticed at the White House, which received tens of thousands. The deluge started immediately after the verdict was announced. By early the following evening, the White House had received 5,505 telegrams and 3,075 telephone calls. All but 5 of the telegrams expressed opposition to the verdict; callers opposed it by a margin estimated at 100 to 1. By 5 April the number of phone calls was up to 8,500 and the number of telegrams to 50,823. In addition, 21,407 letters had been received. Communications on the Calley case continued to run 99 percent against the verdict, and they kept pouring in. A Florida VFW [Veterans of Foreign Wars] leader forwarded the names of a thousand people in his state who wanted the president to help the convicted officer. From Dry Prong, Louisiana, where high school students were reportedly "100% behind Lt. Calley," came petitions urging his release, signed by over 4,500 persons. The mayor of Macon, Georgia, delivered a petition bearing approximately 30,000 signatures, and a disc jockey from Cayce, South Carolina, brought in a duffle bag containing 5,000 letters and "a few thousand more names on petitions." By 13 May the White House had received 260,000 letters and cards and approximately 75,000 telegrams. Over 99 percent of correspondents continued to oppose the verdict. . . .

Calley's Supporters Were Unhappy with the Government

While many factors contributed to the popular lionization of Lieutenant Calley, two were primarily responsible. One was the growing disaffection with the war in Vietnam. Polling data camouflage the connection between the two phenomena. [Psychologist Herbert C.] Kelman and [Lee H.] Lawrence found that those who disapproved of the court-martial were very evenly divided on the war. Twenty-eight percent identified themselves as hawks, 28 percent as doves, and 29 percent as middle-of-the-road. Forty-two percent of respondents to a Louis Harris survey agreed with the proposition that the My Lai incident proved U.S. involvement in Vietnam had been morally wrong all along, while 44 percent disagreed with it. Although these numbers suggest support for Lieutenant Calley was unrelated to feelings about the war, as Tom Huston recognized, "You have two conflicting points of view united in a single conclusion."

Hawks opposed the conviction of Lieutenant Calley because they thought he was being punished simply for waging a war they supported. [Nixon aide Charles] Colson found leaders of veterans' organizations unanimous in the belief that if this was the way America treated its military personnel, it should abandon the struggle in Vietnam immediately. "It is unspeakable that we should be fighting a war and have G.I.'s court-martialed for killing," Mrs. John Schwei of Grand Prairie, Texas, wrote to the Court of Military Appeals. She and other hawks thought Calley was being sent to prison merely for doing his duty. He had not dodged the draft like [Cassius] Clay [also known as "Muhammad Ali"] but instead had volunteered to fight for his country, and now it was punishing him. "This young educated man did not burn his draft card or run away to Canada, but instead became a leader of men in . . . the . . . army," Bill Worthy of Dallas complained to the president. The outpouring of emotion from people like Worthy, as the conservative journal *National Review* recognized, had little to do with Calley himself. What angered hawks was that a soldier was being sanctioned for trying to win the war.

What upset doves, on the other hand, was that Calley was being punished for what they considered the inevitable consequences of a mistaken national policy. "The events of My Lai, for which Lieutenant Calley has been found guilty, are reflective of the tragedy of the entire Vietnam war," wrote Senator Abe Ribicoff (D. Conn.) to the president. The *New Yorker* echoed his sentiments, and Telford Taylor concluded an article entitled "Judging Calley Is Not Enough" by declaring, "It is high time that the people of the United States squarely face the human consequences of their Vietnam venture." All who had supported this policy must share Calley's guilt, Senator Mark Hatfield (R. Ore.) maintained. . . .

Calley's Actions Were Seen As Routine

Although he [Nixon] believed anger over the Calley verdict would rally America behind his program, what it actually did was expand the legions advocating that the war be ended as soon as possible. A Harris poll found that only a bare plurality of Americans (36 percent to 35 percent) considered the lieutenant not guilty and that 53 percent thought his shooting of Vietnamese civilians at My Lai (4)[1] was unjustified (versus 35 percent who viewed it as justified). People believed he should not be held accountable for deeds they regarded as wrong because they considered his actions no different from those of many other American soldiers in Vietnam. The VVAW [Vietnam Veterans Against the War] supported Calley because, as one member of that organization explained, "What he did is what was done on an everyday basis all over Vietnam by every unit. We knew from our own experiences that this was just normal operating procedure." A Gallup poll found only 24 percent of Americans believed My Lai (4) was an isolated episode; 52 percent thought such incidents were common. Eighty-one percent of respondents to a Harris survey were sure similar occurrences had been hidden; only 6 percent disagreed.

To [his supporters] Calley was not a mass murderer but a victim of all that they disliked and distrusted: the war, the "system," and . . . "the Establishment."

The perception that Calley was being punished for conduct that was common in Vietnam drove hawks and doves, for quite different reasons, to the same conclusion. For supporters of the war the outcome of the court-martial was proof that U.S. forces were being kept from doing what they had to do to win; as the *National Review* pointed out, their angry reaction to the verdict was a way of releasing the frustration they felt over being denied victory. A resolution by officials of Artesia, New Mexico, condemning the Calley court-martial, argued that either the use of drafted troops in Vietnam should be halted or "our elected representatives [should] consider taking all necessary steps for the United States to win." In a memorandum to Pat Buchanan on 2 April, [Nixon adviser John] Ehrlichman noted that there was "a strong underlying desire (evidenced by the reaction to the Calley verdict) to get our men and particularly our draftees out of the combat environment." That is, of course, what opponents of the war wanted too. "I . . . think this trial

---

1. There are several My Lai villages in Vietnam. The one that was the site of the massacre in 1968 is designated as number 4.

is additional evidence that our country's involvement in the Indochina conflict must be ended as soon as possible," wrote Senator B. Everett Jordan (D. N.C.) to a constituent. Ironically, Michael Novak noted in *Commonweal,* the outcome of the Calley court-martial seemed "to be crystalizing both hawks and doves in revulsion against the war." As pollster Tom Benham explained to the White House, "the Calley thing" had forced Americans to focus on the negative side of Vietnam and to ask themselves, "What the hell we are doing there?" Two weeks after the verdict, the Harris organization found for the first time that a majority of Americans—56 percent—wanted the war ended and U.S. forces brought home.

People Thought Calley Was a Scapegoat

While the mounting disaffection with the Vietnam War helped rally the public behind Lieutenant Calley, an increase in popular distrust of government was also a factor. Virtually every one thought Calley had been made a scapegoat. In a letter to the Court of Military Appeals, Nancy Cooper, a Fort Worth social studies teacher, called him a "sacrificial lamb." "We realized . . . that Calley was a scapegoat," recalled Joe Urgo of the VVAW, explaining why antiwar veterans supported a convicted murderer. The army denied the little lieutenant was being singled out to bear the entire burden of a difficult war (insisting he was guilty of uniquely infamous atrocities), but the public was not convinced. The military's condemnation of Calley seemed hypocritical and self-serving. Sixty-nine percent of Americans thought he had been singled out unfairly as a scapegoat, a Gallup Poll reported; only 16 percent disagreed. When the Harris organization asked the same question, 77 percent of those it interviewed responded in the affirmative, and just 15 percent answered no. Kelman and Lawrence obtained results nearly identical to Gallup's when they asked whether it was unfair to single out Calley for trial.

Of those Gallup questioned, only 15 percent disapproved of the verdict because they thought no crime had been committed at My Lai (4). Fifty-six percent did so because they believed many others besides Calley shared responsibility for what had happened there. "No one wants to see a single individual saddled with blame that obviously extends to many others," Senator Hughes wrote to President

Nixon. Oscar Schau of Smithfield, Texas, spoke for many Americans when he declared: "Lt. Calley is not guilty, the system is guilty." Forty-nine percent of those the Harris organization questioned thought the army should be blamed for the crimes committed at My Lai (4), whereas only 38 percent thought it should not. If Calley were guilty, then so were "many of his superior officers, some of the higher commanders, and so are our political leaders who helped make the decisions which led to this tragedy," declared several residents of Louisville, Kentucky, in a telegram to the president. A theme running through many of the wires the White House received was that Calley was only a fall guy for others higher up in the chain of command. Asked whether he was being "made the scapegoat for the actions of others above him," 70 percent of those responding to a Gallup survey answered yes; only 12 percent said no. Seventy-seven percent of those questioned by the Harris organization thought the soldiers at My Lai (4) were "only following orders from their higher-ups." Seventy-four percent believed Nixon should either stop all trials such as Calley's or see to it that those higher-ups were tried, too.

These respondents seemed to share the attitude encapsulated in the GI maxim "Shit rolls downhill," a saying that reflected the belief of many soldiers that their leaders could not be trusted and always sought to protect themselves by pushing responsibility for whatever went wrong as far down the chain of command as possible. *The Nation* thought that was what had happened in Calley's case: the army had tried to make a scapegoat out of a lieutenant in order to whitewash its own highest echelons. . . .

People Saw Calley As a Victim of the System

Those who bombarded Congress and the White House with telephone calls and mail and who answered pollsters' questions identified with Calley. He was Everyman. To them Calley was not a mass murderer but a victim of all that they disliked and distrusted: the war, the "system," and what alienated youth referred to pejoratively as "the Establishment." President Nixon recognized how angry the public was, but his efforts to exploit the powerful emotions unleashed by the court-martial of Lieutenant Calley failed because he did not understand the disaffection with the Vietnam War and the resentment of authority that fueled them. Those forces transformed a convicted mass murderer into one of the most improbable heroes in all of American history.

4

The Government Responded Appropriately to the My Lai Massacre

William George Eckhardt

The American massacre of civilian Vietnamese villagers at My Lai in March 1968 was one of the most shocking events of the Vietnam conflict. Once Americans learned of the extent of the massacre and discovered that the army had not seriously investigated the incident for over a year, many began to question the government's response. The army did eventually investigate, and in September 1969 army prosecutors charged Lieutenant William Calley with several counts of premeditated murder. Approximately thirty other officers and enlisted men were ultimately charged, of whom only five were ever tried. Only one perpetrator (Calley) was convicted. So few of the soldiers involved were tried or convicted that it still seemed to many that the army was not doing all that it could to bring the individuals responsible for the massacre to justice.

In this excerpt from an article on the My Lai massacre, William George Eckhardt, the chief prosecutor in the My Lai cases, describes the events at My Lai and defends the government's response to the crimes. Eckhardt argues that the government acted appropriately by trying to prosecute as many perpetrators as possible. He also contends that ultimately the U.S. Army took appropriate action and signaled its disapproval of war crimes by awarding medals to three American soldiers

William George Eckhardt, "My Lai: An American Tragedy," *The Real Lessons of the Vietnam War: Reflections Twenty-Five Years After the Fall of Saigon*, edited by John Norton Moore and Robert F. Turner. Durham, NC: Academic Press, 2002.

who faced down their fellows and saved Vietnamese villagers from the massacre. Eckhardt served in the U.S. Army for over thirty years, retiring as a colonel; he is currently a professor at the University of Missouri–Kansas City Law School.

No one will ever know exactly what happened at My Lai on March 16, 1968. The initial cover-up within the Americal [U.S. Army] Division; the lack of a timely investigation; the absence of physical forensic evidence; the disparity in culture, education, and politics between victims and perpetrators; and the pollution of politics, cause, and national honor make definitive recreation of events impossible. The sources of facts are numerous: news media accounts, journalistic books, the Peers Report (an official investigation), congressional testimony, CID (Police) Reports, and trial testimony. Each of these sources has flaws. Yet, there are common facts that are undeniable and largely undisputed. The basic facts of My Lai are thus not in serious dispute.

Charlie Company of Task Force Barker, a part of the Americal Division, conducted operations in Quang Ngai Province in the Republic of South Vietnam in March of 1968. The My Lai Operation was scheduled for March 16. The area in question, known to the Americans as "Pinkville," was a "hotbed" of enemy activity. Charlie Company, led by Captain Ernest Medina and having Lieutenant William Calley as one of its Platoon Leaders, had been operating in this area and had received several casualties from mines and booby-traps, some undoubtedly planted by civilian Viet Cong sympathizers.

The night before the operation, unfortunately after an emotional memorial service for a respected company casualty, Captain Medina briefed his company on the upcoming operation. This operation was unusual because intelligence indicators pointed, erroneously it turned out, to the presence of a Viet Cong Battalion in the village. A significant engagement was expected. It is widely agreed that Captain Medina gave his Company quite a pep talk. He ordered his men to destroy all crops, kill all livestock, burn all houses, and pollute the water wells of the village. There is, however, an important disagreement concerning his reported orders to kill non-combatants. Significantly, he gave no instructions for their segregation and safeguarding.

After an artillery preparation, Charlie Company was he-
licoptered into the area at 0730 and began a sweep through
the village. Captain Medina remained on the outskirts of
the village so that he could effectively control the operation.
For all practical purposes, there was no resistance. During
the next three hours, houses were burned, livestock killed,
and women were raped and sexually molested. Groups of
villagers were assembled and shot. Especially large groups
of bodies were located in a ditch and beside a trail. In short,
approximately five hundred non-combatants died.

During this period, Captain Medina remained outside
the village, and no evidence placed him at the site of any of
the group killings. He gave an order to conserve ammunition at approximately 0830 in the morning. His Vietnamese
interpreter begged him to stop the killings. He clearly pos-
sessed the ability to communicate with his subordinates and
they with him. When he physically came upon a group of
bodies on a trail, he ordered a cease-fire that was obeyed.
Only a small portion of the soldiers participated in this misconduct. Yet, those who did not participate did not protest
or complain. Captain Medina later told interrogators that
he lost control of his unit and found out "too late" what
took place.

---

*The government merely did its duty and reacted
to a credible, but unusually articulate, citizen's
complaint.*

Circling overhead in a helicopter that morning was
Warrant Officer Hugh Thompson and his two door gunners, Specialists-Four Larry Colburn and Glenn Andreotta.
Puzzlement caused by unusual activity on the ground
turned into alarm and outrage as they realized that Vietnamese civilians were being killed. Hugh Thompson hero-
ically landed his helicopter and ordered his door gunners to
"cover him" as he confronted Lieutenant Calley. Thompson and his men saved civilians who were in a bunker, carried a wounded child to the hospital and vigorously
protested to their superiors. Their efforts resulted in the is-
suance of a cease-fire order from higher headquarters.

During the late afternoon, when queried by higher headquarters and ordered to return to My Lai, Captain Medina gathered his platoon leaders. During that meeting he asked Lieutenant Calley: "How many was it—100 to 200?" Unfortunately, the order to return to the village was countermanded, ostensibly for safety reasons. The tragic day ended as horribly as it began. Captain Medina and an intelligence officer, Captain Eugene Kotouc, interrogated Vietnamese prisoners in conjunction with Vietnamese authorities. Captain Medina shot over the head of a Viet Cong suspect to force him to talk. Captain Kotouc threatened other suspects with a knife, cutting off the finger of one suspect. When Captain Kotouc would point symbolically toward heaven, the accompanying Vietnamese police would lead the suspect away and shoot him.

The Massacre Becomes Public

Public exposure of the My Lai incident did not take place for over a year. An unusually articulate letter triggered an investigation by a former soldier, Ron Ridenhour, to various governmental officials. Yet, it was only after the Army Inspector General had completed his investigation and had turned the probable criminal offenses over to the Criminal Investigation Command for further criminal investigation and after Lieutenant Calley had been formally charged that journalist Seymour Hersh reported the incident. Contrary to the opinions of many public commentators, the press did not expose the incident or cause the government to react. The government merely did its duty and reacted to a credible, but unusually articulate, citizen's complaint.

News media reporting resulted in an instant *cause celebre*. The corroboration of unimaginable allegations and their subsequent investigation riveted America. Pictures of the carnage at My Lai taken by Ronald L. Haeberle, a young Army enlisted reporter during the operation, were published with devastating effect in the December 5, 1969, issue of *Life* magazine. *Time* magazine placed Lieutenant Calley on its cover with a bold caption: "The Massacre: Where Does the Guilt Lie?" The evil of what transpired was further graphically illustrated during a CBS in-person interview with Paul Meadlo, a soldier who assisted Lieutenant Calley. Paul Meadlo emotionally confessed to shooting old men, women, children, and babies.

The Courts-Martial Take Place

Lengthy investigations, hearings, and trials followed. The Criminal Investigation Command, unaided by today's modern computer technology, gathered witness statements from former soldiers scattered across the United States. These reports were the factual basis for prosecution. Lieutenant General William R. Peers was appointed to conduct an inquiry into the incident and its possible causes. His report is a classic government "White Paper," gathering appropriate background information and making necessary individual and institutional assessments. However, the Peers Report's witness statements were largely unhelpful to the trial lawyers. Compound questions coupled with rambling, unfocused answers that often were not pursued provided little trial ammunition. It should be noted that testimony before the House Armed Services Committee was given a congressional classification and was not released prior to the trials. The contents of this congressional testimony played no role in the trials. However, the Armed Service Committee's calculated attempt to block release of this testimony and thus sabotage the criminal trials had a profound impact.

The government . . . formally and publicly admitted the tragic events and publicized for future instruction and emulation the heroic selfless action of an intervener.

The trials that followed were military courts-martial because the accused were soldiers and because the Congress placed "war crimes" exclusively in the military criminal code. Since Congress specifically designed trials by courts-martial to be as similar to criminal trials in civilian federal district courts as possible, the military venue was largely irrelevant to the legal issues involved. "War crimes," in the international law sense, is a technical term. My Lai was not a "war crime" because the victims were not enemy aliens in an occupied territory. Even though not technically "war crimes," what occurred at My Lai clearly fell within the list of crimes specified by Congress in the Uniform Code of Military justice—murder, assault, rape and larceny, among others. These were the crimes chosen for prosecution.

There were two chief locations for these courts-martial: trial for the "ground action" occurred primarily at Fort McPherson, Georgia, and the trial for the "cover-up" at Fort Meade, Maryland. Lieutenant Calley was tried at Fort Benning, Georgia, and Sergeant Mitchell was tried at Fort Hood, Texas, before the cases were consolidated. In all, some thirty individuals were accused of "commission and omission." Charges were preferred against sixteen, five were tried, and one (Lieutenant Calley) was convicted. Charges against twelve others were dismissed prior to trial. This prosecutorial record was abysmal. . .

What Should We Remember About My Lai?

What is the purpose of examining past events? Is not the whole purpose of history to learn from the past to prevent repeating it in the future? One of the most important prosecutorial functions is prevention of similar misconduct. Indeed, the amazing "saga" of My Lai is the willingness of the United States to discuss this institution-staining tragedy and to "use" it to insure professional conduct on the battlefield. The history of the event itself and the problem it represents are critical to the "ending" of this American Tragedy.

The answer to the question, "What should we remember about My Lai?" came with an institutional thunderbolt on March 6, 1998, at the Vietnam Memorial in Washington, D.C., as the Thirtieth Anniversary of this tragedy approached. On that date, the United States Government presented the Soldier's Medal (the highest award for bravery not involving conflict with the enemy) to Hugh Thompson and to his door gunner assistants, Larry Colburn and Glenn Andreotta (posthumously). These three individuals did precisely what soldiers should do: when something went wrong on the battlefield, they intervened to correct it and they reported it.

The *Washington Post* headline says it all: "30 Years Later, Heroes Emerge from Shame of My Lai Massacre." A military medal normally is not presented at a national monument with the Army Band playing, is not attended by dozens of foreign journalists, is not reported in national newspapers with photographs and citations, and is not attended by the Army Chief of Staff and Members of Congress. Yet, thirty years after this tragic incident, the government publicly and permanently acknowledged what transpired and took steps to insure that in remembering and in teaching this tragedy, the appropriate conduct exemplified by Hugh Thompson and his crew would become an essential lesson. Although Lieutenant William Calley's actions will always be remembered with horror, shame, and revulsion, the selfless, professional actions of Hugh Thompson and his assistants should not only be remembered, but emulated.

The tone and purpose of this ceremony began with an invocation, prominently reported by *The New York Times*: "We stand in honor of their heroism, and we have taken too long to recognize them. Remembering a dark point in time, we are now a richer nation as their personal heroic service is woven into the fabric of our history." Nothing could be more important than to honor the moral courage represented by Hugh Thompson. He is the Sir Thomas More [the Englishman who died rather than accept what he saw as the hypocrisy of the King] of our current military. Life-risking action to perform the basic duty of a soldier, protecting the defenseless, coupled with the moral courage to report and to testify, mark him as someone to emulate. My personal admiration knows no bounds for the additional moral courage that is *not* reflected in the citation. Hugh Thompson, over the course of some two years during the My Lai hearings, told the truth despite peer pressure, ostracism, threats of prosecution, and a nationally televised congressional brow-beating. All of these acts were an attempt to prevent him from testifying or to punish him for doing so.

The Government Has Acted Correctly

The most fitting official end of the My Lai "saga" is the approved governmental wording in the citation for the Soldier's Medal awarded to Hugh Thompson. This is the My Lai of history:

> For heroism above and beyond the call of duty on 16 March 1968, while saving the lives of at least 10 Vietnamese civilians during the unlawful massacre of noncombatants by American forces at My Lai, Quang Ngai province, South Vietnam. Warrant Officer Thompson landed his helicopter in the line of fire between fleeing Vietnamese civilians and pursuing American ground troops to prevent their murder. He then personally confronted the leader of the American

ground troops and was prepared to open fire on those American troops should they fire upon the civilians. Warrant Officer Thompson, at the risk of his own personal safety, went forward of the American lines and coaxed the Vietnamese civilians out of the bunker to enable their evacuation. Leaving the area after requesting and overseeing the civilians' air evacuation, his crew spotted movement in a ditch filled with bodies south of My Lai Four. Warrant Officer Thompson again landed his helicopter and covered his crew as they retrieved a wounded child from the pile of bodies. He then flew the child to the safety of a hospital at Quang Ngai. Warrant Officer Thompson's relayed radio reports of the massacre and subsequent report to his section leader and commander resulted in an order for the cease-fire at My Lai and an end to the killing of innocent civilians. Warrant Officer Thompson's heroism exemplified the highest standards of personal courage and ethical conduct, reflecting distinct credit on him and the United States Army.

Most importantly, the Army, the very institution shamed by My Lai, has explicitly and prominently heralded Hugh Thompson's battlefield example in its all important leadership guide. The Army's Field Manual notes that "[i]n combat physical and moral courage may blend together. The right thing to do may not only be unpopular, but dangerous as well. Situations of that sort reveal who's a leader of character and who's not." Prominently displayed across the whole printed page is the Hugh Thompson Example.

Thus, a prosecutor's duty is concluded. The government investigated and did not cover-up. The government publicly condemned the atrocity and persistently prosecuted despite unprecedented odds. The government focused on this horrible lesson and, in the corrective actions that followed, significantly advanced the Law of War. The government, assisted by the passage of time, formally and publicly admitted the tragic events and publicized for future instruction and emulation the heroic selfless action of an intervener. The prosecution lesson for the future is clear. ACT LIKE HUGH THOMPSON.

Chapter 3

Vietnamese War Crimes

1

The Vietnamese
Committed War Crimes
During the Tet Offensive

Douglas Pike

In January 1968, just as most Americans were beginning to believe that the war in Vietnam was coming to a gradual (and vic-
torious) close, the North Vietnamese and the Vietcong
launched a massive surprise attack. This attack, coming as it
did on the Tet holiday, was known as the "Tet Offensive." The
Tet Offensive was a tactical disaster for the Vietnamese Communists. However, the North Vietnamese did manage to capture the South Vietnamese city of Hue and hold it for some
time before being driven out on February 26, 1968.

In the aftermath of the battle for Hue, residents and South
Vietnamese and American troops discovered a number of shal-
low mass graves near the city. Journalists reported that many
of the dead had been tied up with telephone wire, had been
tortured before death, and appeared to have been executed.
Most observers in the United States concluded that the North
Vietnamese and their Vietcong allies had committed atrocities
at Hue and were guilty of war crimes. One of the most influential proponents of this theory was Douglas Eugene Pike, an
American foreign service officer. In 1970 Pike published an
eighty-eight-page booklet entitled *The Viet Cong Strategy of
Terror*, in which he presented evidence of what he argued was
the Communist massacre in Hue. In this excerpt, Pike summa-
rizes some of that evidence and presents his hypothesis of how
the killings unfolded.

After leaving government service, Pike authored several
highly regarded books on the North Vietnamese. In 1997 he

Douglas Pike, *The Viet Cong Strategy of Terror*. Saigon, U.S. Mission, Vietnam,
1970.

brought his massive collection of Vietnam-era documents to the Vietnam Center at Texas Tech University, where he remained as associate director of research until his death in 2002.

The city of Hue is one of the saddest cities of our earth, not simply because of what happened there in February, 1968, unthinkable as that was. It is a silent rebuke to all of us, inheritors of 40 centuries of civilization, who in our century have allowed collectivist politics to corrupt us into the worst of the modern sins, indifference to inhumanity. What happened in Hue should give pause to every civilized person. It should be inscribed, so as not to be forgotten, along with the record of other terrible visitations of man's inhumanity to man which stud the history of the human race. Hue is another demonstration of what man can bring himself to do when he fixes no limits on political action and pursues uncautiously the dream of social perfectibility.

What happened in Hue, physically, can be described with a few quick statistics. A communist force which eventually reached 12,000 invaded the city the night of the new moon marking the new lunar year, January 30, 1968. It stayed for 26 days and then was driven out by military action. In the wake of this Tet offensive, 5,800 Hue civilians were dead or missing. It is now known that most of them are dead. The bodies of most have been found in the past 20 months, in single and mass graves throughout Thua Thien province which surrounds this cultural capital of Viet-Nam.

Hue is another demonstration of what man can bring himself to do when he fixes no limits on political action and pursues uncautiously the dream of social perfectibility.

Such are the skeletal facts, the important statistics. Such is what the incurious world knows, if it knows anything at all about Hue, for this is what was written, modestly, by the world's press. Apparently it made no impact on the world's mind or conscience. For there was no agonized outcry. No demonstrations at North Vietnamese embassies around the world. Lord [Bertrand] Russel [founder of an International War Crimes Tribunal] did not send his "war crimes tribunal" to Hue to take evidence and indict. In a tone beyond bitterness, the people there will tell you that the world does not know what happened in Hue or if it does, does not care. . . .

Discovering the Bodies

In the chaos that existed following the battle, the first order of civilian business was emergency relief, in the form of food shipments, prevention of epidemics, emergency medical care, etc. Then came the home rebuilding effort. Only later did Hue begin to tabulate its casualties. No true post-attack census has yet been taken. In March local officials reported that 1,900 civilians were hospitalized with war wounds and they estimated that some 5,800 persons were unaccounted for.

In all almost 1,200 bodies were found in hastily dug, poorly concealed graves. At least half of these showed clear evidence of atrocity killings.

The first discovery of communist victims came in the Gia Hoi High School yard, on February 26; eventually 170 bodies were recovered. In the next few months 18 additional grave sites were found, the largest of which were Tang Quang Tu Pagoda (67 victims), Bai Dau (77), Cho Thong area (an estimated 100), the imperial tombs area (201), Thien Ham (approximately 200), and Dong Gi (approximately 100). In all almost 1,200 bodies were found in hastily dug, poorly concealed graves. At least half of these showed clear evidence of atrocity killings: hands wired behind backs, rags stuffed in mouths, bodies contorted but without wounds (indicating burial alive). The other nearly 600 bore wound marks but there was no way of determining whether they died by firing squad or incidental to the battle. Among these victims were three West German doctors, a medical technician who was the wife of one of the doctors, and two French Catholic priests, one of whom was buried alive.

The second major group of finds was discovered in the first seven months of 1969 in Phu Thu district—the Sand Dune Finds and Le Xa Tay—and Huong Thuy district—

Xuan Hoa-Van Duong—in late March and April. Additional grave sites were found in Vinh Loc district in May and in Nam Hoa district in July.

The largest of this group were the Sand Dune Finds in the three sites of Vinh Luu, Le Xa Dong and Xuan O located in rolling, grass-tufted sand dune country near the South China Sea. Separated by salt-marsh valleys, these dunes were ideal for graves.

On the discovery of the Sand Dune Finds a story is told that a local farmer, walking over the dunes one morning, tripped over a piece of wire sticking out of the sand. In ire he jerked at the wire and out of the sand, at the other end of his wire, came a bony hand and arm. The find was made. Excavation work was ordered, and 809 bodies were uncovered.

Excavating the Bodies Carefully

A fixed procedure then developed, now used in all the excavations. Four-person teams, usually young people, operate as a unit. They wear surgical gloves well-doused in alcohol, their faces masked to avoid odor. They dig systematically, using sound archeological principles. The area is marked off into a grid. Digging is done with flat shovels used in a peculiar sideward motion that slices away layer after layer of sand until a strike is made. Then, with the aid of a small garden trowel, the body is uncovered. It is removed and placed on a sheet of plastic. Then comes registration: a number painted on the skull and a description (dental impression, color of hair, identifying papers, clothing, jewelry, religious artifacts, etc.) listed in a record book. The body is then carted away to a central clearing station where the information gathered is posted before waiting relatives. It is slow work, averaging six man-hours per body.

The teams are now experienced and even specialized. Some are assigned the task of probing the sand with long iron rods and have developed an almost sixth sense as to where the bodies are. Others specialize in removing bodies intact, important in terms of later identification. One old man has gained fame for his ability to identify persons he has known by the shape and feel of skulls.

Vegetation is one indicator, the presence of bright green grass is an almost certain sign that a body is beneath. Young children are another source of information. A fourteen-year-old buffalo boy with a sharp eye and a good memory pinpointed the location of more than a dozen bodies, which he had watched the communists bury a year and a half ago.

What the Bodies Showed

In the Sand Dune Find, the pattern had been to tie victims together in groups of 10 or 20, line them up in front of a trench dug by local corvee labor and cut them down with submachine gun (a favorite local souvenir is a spent Russian machine gun shell taken from a grave). Frequently the dead were buried in layers of three and four, which makes identification particularly difficult.

In Nam Hoa district came the third, or Da Mai Creek Find, which also has been called the Phu Cam death march, made on September 19, 1969. Three communist defectors told intelligence officers of the 101st Airborne Brigade that they had witnessed the killing of several hundred people at Da Mai Creek, about 10 miles south of Hue, in February of 1968. The area is wild, unpopulated, virtually inaccessible. The Brigade sent a search party, which reported that the stream contained a large number of human bones.

By piecing together bits of information, it was determined that this is what happened at Da Mai Creek: On the fifth day of Tet in the Phu Cam section of Hue, where some three-fourths of the City's 40,000 Roman Catholics lived, a large number of people had taken sanctuary from the battle in a local church, a common method in Viet-Nam of escaping war. Many in the building were not in fact Catholic. A communist political commissar arrived at the church and ordered out about 400 people, some by name and some apparently because of their appearance (prosperous looking and middle-aged businessmen, for example). He said they were going to the "liberated area" for three days of indoctrination, after which each could return home. They were marched nine kilometers south to a pagoda where the communists had established a headquarters. There 20 were called out from the group, assembled before a drumhead court, tried, found guilty, executed and buried in the pagoda yard. The remainder were taken across the river and turned over to a local communist unit in an exchange that even involved handing the political commissar a receipt. It is probable that the commissar intended that their prisoners should be re-educated and returned, but with the turnover, matters passed from his control. During the next several days, exactly how many is not known, both captive and captor wandered the countryside. At some point in Phase III (see below) the local communists decided to eliminate witnesses. Their captives were led through six kilometers of some of the most rugged terrain in Central Viet-Nam, to Da Mai Creek. There they were shot or brained and their bodies left to wash in the running stream.

The Killings Were Meant to Be Secret

The 101st Airborne Brigade burial detail found it impossible to reach the creek overland, roads being non-existent or impassable. The creek's foliage is what in Viet-Nam is called double-canopy, that is, two layers, one consisting of brush and trees close to the ground, and the second of tall trees whose branches spread out high above. Beneath is permanent twilight. Brigade engineers spent two days blasting a hole through the double-canopy by exploding dynamite dangled on lens wires beneath their hovering helicopters. This cleared a landing pad for helicopter hearses. Quite clearly this was a spot where death could be easily hidden even without burial.

The Da Mai Creek bed, for nearly a hundred yards up the ravine, yielded skulls, skeletons and pieces of human bones. The dead had been left above ground (for the animists among them, this meant their souls would wander the lonely earth forever, since such is the fate of the unburied dead), and 20 months in the running stream had left bones clean and white.

The story remains uncompleted. If the estimates by Hue officials are even approximately correct, nearly 2,000 people are still missing.

Local authorities later released a list of 428 names of persons whom they said had been positively identified from the creek bed remains.

The fourth or Phu Thu Salt Flat Finds came in November 1969, near the fishing village of Luong Vien some ten miles east of Hue, another desolate region. Government troops early in the month began an intensive effort to clear the area of remnants of the local communist organization.

People of Luong Vien, population 700, who had remained silent in the presence of troops for 20 months apparently felt secure enough from communist revenge to break silence and lead officials to the find. At this writing, excavation work is under way. Based on descriptions from villagers whose memories are not always clear, local officials estimate the number of bodies at Phu Thu to be at least 300 and possibly 1,000.

The story remains uncompleted. If the estimates by Hue officials are even approximately correct, nearly 2,000 people are still missing. . . .

The Communist Rationale for Killing

The killing in Hue that added up to the Hue Massacre far exceeded in numbers any atrocity by the communists previously in South Viet-Nam. The difference was not only one in degree but one in kind. The character of the terror that emerges from an examination of Hue is quite distinct from communist terror acts elsewhere, frequent or brutal as they may have been. The . . . objectives for communist terror scarcely fit for Hue. The terror in Hue was not a morale building act—the quick blow deep into the enemy's lair which proves enemy vulnerability and the guerrilla's omnipotence and which is quite different from gunning down civilians in areas under guerrilla control. Nor was it terror to advertise the cause. Nor to disorient and psychologically isolate the individual, since the vast majority of the killings were done secretly. Nor . . . was it terror to eliminate opposing forces. Hue did not follow the pattern of terror to provoke governmental over-response since it resulted in only what might have been anticipated—government assistance. There were elements of each objective, true, but none serves to explain the widespread and diverse pattern of death meted out by the communists.

What is offered here is a hypothesis which will suggest logic and system behind what appears to be simple, random slaughter. Before dealing with it, let us consider three facts which constantly reassert themselves to a Hue visitor seeking to discover what exactly happened there and, more importantly, exactly *why* it happened. All three fly in the face of common sense and contradict to a degree what has been written. Yet, in talking to all sources—province chief, police chief, American advisor, eye witness, captured prisoner, *hoi chanh* (defector) or those few who miraculously escaped a death scene—these three facts emerge again and again.

These Were Not Random Killings

The first fact, and perhaps the most important, is that despite contrary appearances virtually no communist killing was due to rage, frustration, or panic during the communist withdrawal at the end. Such explanations are frequently heard, but they fail to hold up under scrutiny. Quite the contrary, to trace back any single killing is to discover that almost without exception it was the result of a decision rational and justifiable in the communist mind. In fact, most killings were, from the communist calculation, imperative.

The second fact is that, as far as can be determined, virtually all killings were done by local communists cadres and not by the PAVN [People's Army of Vietnam (North Vietnamese army)] troops or Northerners or other outside communists. Some 12,000 PAVN troops fought the battle of Hue and killed civilians in the process but this was incidental to their military effort. Most of the 150 communist civilian cadres operating within the city were local, that is from the Thua Thien province area. They were the ones who issued the death orders. Whether they acted on instructions from higher headquarters (and the communist organizational system is such that one must assume they did), and, if so, what exactly those orders were, no one yet knows for sure.

The third fact is that beyond "example" executions of prominent "tyrants", most of the killings were done secretly with extraordinary effort made to hide the bodies. Most outsiders have a mental picture of Hue as a place of public executions and prominent mass burial mounds of fresh-turned earth. Only in the early days were there well-publicized executions and these were relatively few. The burial sites in the city were easily discovered because it is difficult to create a graveyard in a densely populated area without someone noticing it. All the other finds were well hidden, all in terrain lending itself to concealment, probably the reason the sites were chosen in the first place. A body in the sand dunes is as difficult to find as a sea shell pushed deep into a sandy beach over which a wave has washed. Da Mai Creek is in the remotest part of the province and must have required great exertion by the communists to lead their victims there. Had not the three *hoi chanh* led searchers to the wild uninhabited spot the bodies might well remain undiscovered to this day. A visit to all sites leaves one with the impression that the communists made a major effort to hide their deeds.

The hypothesis offered here connects and fixes in time the communist assessment of their prospects for staying in Hue with the kind of death order issued. It seems clear from sifting evidence that they had no single unchanging assessment with regard to themselves and their future in Hue, but rather that changing situations during the course of the battle altered their prospects and their intentions. It also seems equally clear from the evidence that there was no single communist policy on death orders; instead the kind of death order issued changed during the course of the battle. The correlation between these two is high and divides into three phases. The hypothesis therefore is that *as communist plans during the Battle of Hue changed so did the nature of the death orders issued.* This conclusion is based on overt communist statements, testimony by prisoners and *hoi chanh*, accounts of eye witnesses, captured documents and the internal logic of the communist situation. . . .

Phase I of Killing

During the brief stay in Hue, the civilian cadres, accompanied by execution squads, were to round up and execute key individuals whose elimination would greatly weaken the government's administrative apparatus following communist withdrawal. This was the blacklist period, the time of the drumhead court. Cadres with lists of names and addresses on clipboard appeared and called into kangaroo court various "enemies of the Revolution." Their trials were public, usually in the courtyard of a temporary communist headquarters. The trials lasted about ten minutes each and there are no known not-guilty verdicts. Punishment, invariably execution, was meted out immediately. Bodies were either hastily buried or turned over to relatives. Singled out for this treatment were civil servants, especially those involved in security or police affairs, military officers and some non-commissioned officers, plus selected non-official but natural leaders of the community, chiefly educators and religionists.

With the exception of a particularly venomous attack on Hue intellectuals, the Phase I pattern was standard operating procedure for communists in Viet-Nam. It was the sort of thing that had been going on systematically in the villages for ten years. Permanent blacklists, prepared by zonal or inter-zone Party headquarters have long existed for use throughout the country, whenever an opportunity presents itself. Quite obviously not all the people named in the lists used in Hue were liquidated. One meets today a surprisingly large number of people who obviously were listed, who stayed in the city throughout the battle, but escaped. Throughout the 24-day period the communist cadres were busy hunting down persons on their blacklists, but after a few days their major efforts were turned into a new channel.

Phase II of Killing

In the first few days, the Tet offensive affairs progressed so well for the communists in Hue (although not to the south, where Party chiefs received some rather grim evaluations from cadres in the midst of the offensive in the Mekong Delta) that for a brief euphoric moment they believed they could hold the city. Probably the assessment that the communist were in Hue to stay was not shared at the higher echelons. . . .

But testimony from prisoners and *hoi chanh*, as well as intercepted battle messages, indicate that both rank and file and cadres believed for a few days they were permanently in Hue, and they acted accordingly.

Among their acts was to extend the death order and launch what in effect was a period of social reconstruction, communist style. Orders went out, apparently from the provincial level of the Party, to round up what one prisoner termed "social negatives," that is, those individuals or members of groups who represented potential danger or liability in the new social order. This was quite impersonal, not a blacklist of names but a blacklist of titles and positions held in the old society, directed not against people as such but against "social units.". . .

The killings in Phase II perhaps accounted for 2,000 of the missing. But the worst was not yet over.

Phase III of Killing

Inevitably, and as the leadership in Hanoi must have assumed all along, considering the forces ranged against it, the battle in Hue turned against the communist. An intercepted PAVN radio message from the Citadel [the site of the old Imperial Vietnamese palace], February 22, asked for permission to withdraw. Back came the reply: permission refused, attack on the 23rd. That attack was made, a last, futile one. On the 24th the Citadel was taken.

That expulsion was inevitable was apparent to the communists for at least the preceding week. It was then that began Phase III, the cover-the-traces period. Probably the entire civilian underground *apparat* in Hue had exposed itself during Phase II. Those without suspicion rose to proclaim their identity. Typical is the case of one Hue resident who described his surprise on learning that his next door neighbor was the leader of a phuong (which made him 10th to 15th ranking communist civilian in the city), saying in wonder, "I'd know him for 18 years and never thought he was the least interested in politics." Such a cadre could not go underground again unless there was no one around who remembered him.

Hence Phase III, elimination of witnesses.

Probably the largest number of killings came during this period and for this reason. Those taken for political indoctrination probably were slated to be returned. But they were local people as were their captors; names and faces were familiar. So, as the end approached they became not just a burden but a positive danger. Such undoubtedly was the case with the group taken from the church at Phu Cam. Or of the 15 high school students whose bodies were found as part of the Phu Thu Salt Flat find.

Categorization in a hypothesis such as this is, of course, gross and at best only illustrative. Things are not that neat in real life. For example, throughout the entire time the blacklist hunt went on. Also, there was revenge killing by the communists in the name of the Party, the so-called "revolutionary justice." And undoubtedly there were personal vendettas, old scores settled by individual Party members. (How else can one explain one body found at Phu Thu in which every principal bone had been broken?) . . .

The Moral of the Massacre

The meaning of the Hue Massacre seems clear. If the communists win decisively in South Viet-Nam (and the key word is decisively), what is the prospect? First, all foreigners would be cleared out of the South, especially the hundreds of foreign newsmen who are in and out of Saigon. A curtain of ignorance would descend. Then would begin a night of long knives.[1] There would be a new order to build. The war was long and so are memories of old scores to be settled. All political opposition, actual or potential, would be systematically eliminated. . . . Beyond this would come communist justice meted out to the "tyrants and lackeys." Personal revenge would be a small wheel turning within the larger wheel of Party retribution.

But little of this would be known abroad. The communists in Viet-Nam would create a silence.

The world would call it peace.

---

1. A reference to Adolf Hitler's 1934 purge of Nazi leadership.

The United States Lied About North Vietnamese War Crimes During Tet

D. Gareth Porter

Some historians, including Douglas Pike, argue that during the 1968 Tet Offensive the North Vietnamese attempted to secure their position in the captured city of Hue by rounding up and executing many South Vietnamese opponents of the Communist North. While journalistic reports of mass graves tend to support Pike's allegations, other historians, including many who opposed U.S. involvement in Southeast Asia and supported the Communist revolution in North Vietnam, claim that the bodies discovered in Hue were victims of the fighting and of indiscriminate American bombing. In this excerpt from a 1974 article in the *Indochina Chronicle*, historian D. Gareth Porter argues that the so-called Communist massacre at Hue is one of the "enduring myths" of the Vietnam conflict and calls the contention that the North Vietnamese carried out indiscriminate executions a "complete fabrication." Porter, who sympathized with North Vietnam, claims that the United States was simply trying to spread anti-Communist propaganda by claiming a massacre had taken place. In Porter's view, Douglas Pike himself was one of the leading figures behind U.S. efforts to lie and "spin" the story of what happened at Hue.

Always a controversial figure, D. Gareth Porter became even more controversial in the mid-1970s when he defended the Khmer Rouge, the Communist revolutionaries who took power in Cambodia, even after it became apparent that they had orchestrated the systematic torture and executions of literally millions of Cambodians. Porter is currently an analyst for Foreign Policy in Focus and is the author of several books, including *Cambodia: Starvation and Revolution* (with George C. Hildebrand) and *Perils of Dominance: Imbalance of Power and the Road to War in Vietnam.*

Six years after the stunning communist Tet Offensive of 1968, one of the enduring myths of the Second Indochina War remains essentially unchallenged: the communist "massacre" at Hue. The official version of what happened in Hue has been that the National Liberation Front (NLF) and the North Vietnamese deliberately and systematically murdered not only responsible officials but religious figures, the educated elite and ordinary people, and that burial sites later found yielded some 3,000 bodies, the largest portion of the total of more than 4,700 victims of communist execution.

Although there is still much that is not known about what happened in Hue, there is sufficient evidence to conclude that the story conveyed to the American public by South Vietnamese and American propaganda agencies bore little resemblance to the truth, but was, on the contrary, the result of a political warfare campaign by the Saigon government, embellished by the U.S. government and accepted uncritically by the U.S. press. A careful study of the official story of the Hue "massacre" on the one hand, and of the evidence from independent or anti-communist sources on the other, provides a revealing glimpse into efforts by the U.S. press to keep alive fears of a massive "bloodbath."[1] It is a myth which has served U.S. administration interests well in the past, and continues to influence public attitudes deeply today. . . .

Douglas Pike's Propaganda

It was in large part due to the work of one man that the Hue "massacre" received significant press coverage and wide comment in 1969 and 1970. That man was the U.S. Infor-

---

1. Many policy experts argued that a U.S. withdrawal from Vietnam would result in a bloodbath in which communists would execute large numbers of noncommunist Vietnamese.

mation Agency's Douglas Pike. It was Pike who visited South Vietnam in November 1969, apparently at the suggestion of Ambassador Ellsworth Bunker, to prepare a report on Hue.

During the last two weeks of November, Pike inspired, either directly or indirectly, several different newspaper articles on both Hue and the "bloodbath" theme in general. Pike himself briefed several reporters on his version of the communist occupation of Hue and at the same time circulated a translation of a captured communist document which he had found in the files and which he argued was an open admission of the mass murder of innocent civilians during the occupation of Hue.

The document was the subject of several stories in the American press. The *Washington Post*, for example, carried the Associated Press article on the document with the headline, "Reds Killed 2,900 in Hue during Tet, according to Seized Enemy Document." The *Christian Science Monitor* correspondent's article, under the headline, "Communists Admit Murder," began, "The Communist massacre in Hue in early 1968 represented the culmination of careful planning." Both articles quoted as proof of the "admission" the following sentence from the translation: "We eliminated 1,892 administrative personnel, 39 policemen, 790 tyrants, 6 captains, 2 first lieutenants, 20 second lieutenants and many non-commissioned officers."

Misreading a Document

No reporter questioned the authenticity of the document or the accuracy of the translation they were given. Yet the original Vietnamese document, a copy of which I obtained from the U.S. Command in Vietnam in September 1972, shows that the anonymous author did not say what the press and public were led to believe he said. In the original Vietnamese, the sentence quoted above does not support the official U.S. line that the communists admitted murdering more than 2,600 civilians in Hue. To begin with, the context in which this sentence was written was not a discussion of punishing those who were considered criminals or "enemies," but an overall account of the offensive in destroying the army and administration in Thua Thien. Two paragraphs earlier, the document refers to the establishment of a "political force whose mission was to propagandize and appeal for enemy soldiers to surrender with their weapons." It recalls that self-defense forces were so frightened when the [National Liberation] Front's forces attacked that they tried to cross the river, with the result that 21 of them drowned. The section dealing with Phu Vang district notes the strength of the opposing forces and the locus of the attack, claiming the seizure of 12 trucks to transport food and 60 rolls of cloth for flags.

One of the enduring myths of the Second Indochina War remains essentially unchallenged: the communist "massacre" at Hue.

It is the next sentence which says, "We eliminated 1,892 administrative personnel" in the official translation. But the word *diêt*, translated as "eliminate" here, must be understood to mean "destroy" or "neutralize" in a military sense, rather than to "kill" or "liquidate," as Pike and the press reports claimed. As used in communist military communiques, the term had previously been used to include killed, wounded or captured among enemy forces. For example, the Third Special Communique of the People's Liberation Armed Forces, issued at the end of the Tet Offensive, said, "We have destroyed [*diêt*] a large part of the enemy's force; according to initial statistics, we have killed, wounded and captured more than 90,000 enemy. . . ." It should be noted that *diêt* does not mean to "kill" in any ordinary Vietnamese usage, and that the official translation is highly irregular.

Moreover, the word *te*, translated as "administrative personnel" in the version circulated to newsmen, actually has the broader meaning, according to a standard North Vietnamese dictionary, of "puppet personnel," including both civilian *and* military. When the document does refer specifically to the Saigon government's administration, in fact, it uses a different term, *nguy quyen*. Both the context and the normal usage of the words in question, therefore, belie the meaning which Pike successfully urged on the press. . . .

Pike Exaggerated the Numbers

The major accomplishment of Pike's work was to launch the official "estimate" of 4,756 as the number of civilians killed by the NLF in and around Hue. This was no small feat because, in arriving at that figure, Pike had to statistically conjure away thousands of civilian victims of American air power in Hue. The undeniable fact was that American rockets and bombs, not communist assassination, caused the greatest carnage in Hue. The bloodshed and ruin shook even longtime supporters of the anti-communist effort. Robert Shaplen wrote at the time, "Nothing I saw during the Korean War, or in the Vietnam War so far has been as terrible, in terms of destruction and despair, as what I saw in Hue. After the communist occupation had ended, Don Tate of Scripps-Howard Newspapers described bomb craters 40 feet wide and 20 feet deep staggered in the streets near the walls of the citadel and "bodies stacked into graves by fives—one on top of another." Nine thousand seven hundred and seventy-six of Hue's 17,134 houses were completely destroyed and 3,169 more officially classified as "seriously damaged." (In the rest of Thua Thien province another 8,000 homes were more than half destroyed.) The initial South Vietnamese estimate of the number of civilians killed in the fighting of the bloody reconquest was 3,776.

The undeniable fact was that American rockets and bombs, not communist assassination, caused the greatest carnage in Hue.

When ARVN's [Army of the Republic of Vietnam, the South Vietnamese Army] political warfare specialists went to work, however, this initial estimate, given in a March 1968 report of the office of the provincial chief of Social Services and Refugees, was somehow replaced by a new estimate of 944, published in the [ARVN] Tenth Political Warfare Battalion's booklet. And this was all Douglas Pike needed to transform those thousands of civilian dead into victims of a "communist massacre."

In a chart which he calls a "recapitulation" of the dead and missing, Pike begins not by establishing the number of casualties from various causes, but with a total of 7,600, which he says is the Saigon government's "total estimated civilian casualties resulting from the Battle of Hue." The original government estimate of civilian casualties, however, again supplied by the provincial Social Services Office, was just over 6,700—not 7,600—and it was based on the estimate of 3,776 civilians killed in the battle of Hue. Instead of using the Social Services Office's figure, Pike employs the Political Warfare Battalion's 944 figure. Subtracting that number and another 1,900 hospitalized with war wounds, Pike gets the figure of 4,756, which he suggests is the total number of victims of communist massacre, including the 1,945 "unaccounted for" in this strange method of accounting. In short, the whole statistical exercise had the sole purpose of arriving at a fraudulent figure of 4,756 victims of a "massacre."

Pike's Controversial Hypothesis

The substance of Pike's own analysis is what he calls a "hypothesis" concerning the policy of the NLF leadership in Hue during the occupation of the city. The gist of the "hypothesis" is as follows: NLF policy went through three distinct phases, corresponding to different phases of the occupation: in the first few days, the NLF expected to be in control only temporarily and its mission was not to establish its own government but to destroy the Saigon administrative structure. During this period, NLF cadres with blacklists executed not only civil servants and military officers but religious and social leaders as well. Then, after the third or fourth day, the communist leadership decided they could hold the city permanently, whereupon they launched a "period of social reconstruction," in Pike's words, and sought to kill all who were not proletarian in ideology and class background, in particular Buddhist, Catholic and intellectual leaders. Finally, as they prepared to leave the city late in February, they killed anyone who would be able to identify their cadres in the city.

The screen of falsehood which has been erected around the Tet Offensive in Hue was and is but another defense mechanism for the U.S. government.

While Pike refers vaguely to various pieces of evidence which he claims support this hypothesis, he offers none of it in his published work. In any case, all the evidence available at present contradicts Pike's hypothesis from beginning to end. To begin with, captured NLF documents indicate that the Front had the mission not only of destroying the Saigon administration but of establishing a revolutionary government in Hue and planned to hold the city for as long as possible. In fact, the very document which Pike used to establish the communist admission of responsibility for mass murder of civilians specified that the Liberation Forces had the "mission of occupying Hue as long as possible so that a revolutionary administration could be established."

As for the "blacklists" for execution, Pike's claim that the list was extensive and included lower-ranking officials and non-governmental figures is contradicted by none other than Hue's chief of secret police, Le Ngan, whose own name was on the list. In 1968, soon after the reoccupation of the city, Le Ngan told former International Voluntary Services worker Len Ackland, who had worked in Hue before the offensive, that the only names on the blacklist for Gia Hoi district were those of the officers of the secret police apparatus for the district.

Enemies Were to Be Captured, Not Killed

Other lists were of those selected not for summary execution but for capture on the one hand and for reeducation in place on the other. Those who were to be captured—although not necessarily executed, according to a document called "Plan for an Offensive and General Uprising of Mui A" given to me by the Joint U.S. Public Affairs Office in June 1971—were limited to a relatively small number of Vietnamese and American officials. The document says, "With regard to the province chief, deputy province chief, officers from the rank of major up, American intelligence officers and chiefs of services, if things go to our advantage, at 12 o'clock on the day some of them are arrested, they must quickly persuade others not to hide and compel them to surrender . . . and then we must take them out of the city." The captives were to remain in prison outside the city, according to the plan, until their dossiers could be studied and a determination made on their individual cases. It emphasized that none of these higher U.S. or Vietnamese officials in Hue was to be killed unless the fighting in the first hours was unsuccessful and there was no way to conduct them out of the city—a circumstance which obviously did not arise.

The document further exempted lower-ranking officials from capture or retribution: "With regard to those ordinary civil servants working for the enemy because of their livelihood and who do not oppose the revolution, educate them and quickly give them responsibility to continue working to serve the revolution."

There was a third category of individual, those who were neither high-ranking officials nor ordinary civil servants but officials who had at one time or another been involved actively in the government's paramilitary apparatus. While these individuals were not to be given jobs, the evidence indicates that they were to be "reeducated" rather than executed as long as the NLF was assured of control of the city. They were ordered in the first days of the occupation to report to their local committees but were then allowed to return home.

This does not mean that there were no executions in Hue during the initial period of the occupation. Len Ackland and *Washington Post* correspondent Don Oberdorfer have documented cases of individuals who were executed when they tried to hide from the Front or resisted the new government in some other way. But these harsh measures, which may in many cases have reflected individual actions by soldiers or cadres rather than a policy decision by the Front (as when a person was shot resisting arrest), were distinct from the mass retribution for official position or political attitude claimed by Douglas Pike. And the number of executions was relatively small, according to Hue residents interviewed by Ackland. . . .

The Events at Hue Are American Propaganda

Pike's "hypothesis," therefore, must be judged unworthy of serious consideration. It represents ill-informed speculation undisciplined by attention to the available documentary evidence, much less to the revolutionary strategy and tactics about which Pike claims to be an expert. Yet Pike's pamphlet must be considered a political warfare success, for his interpretation of events in Hue remains the dominant one for journalists and public figures.

The issue which historians must weigh in the NLF occupation of Hue is not whether executions took place but whether they were indiscriminate or the result of a prearranged "purge" of whole strata of society, as charged by political warfare specialists of the Saigon and U.S. governments. Equally important is the question of whether it was the NLF or U.S. bombing and artillery which caused the deaths of several thousand Hue civilians during the battle for the city.

The available evidence—not from NLF sources but from official U.S. and Saigon documents and from independent observers—indicates that the official story of an indiscriminate slaughter of those who were considered to be unsympathetic to the NLF is a complete fabrication. Not only is the number of bodies uncovered in and around Hue open to question, but more important, the cause of death appears to have been shifted from the fighting itself to NLF execution. And the most detailed and "authoritative" account of the alleged executions put together by either government does not stand up under examination.

Understanding the techniques of distortion and misrepresentation practiced by Saigon and U.S. propagandists in making a political warfare campaign out of the tragedy of Hue is as important today as it was when U.S. troops were still at war in Vietnam. It goes to the heart of the problem of facing the truth about the Vietnamese revolution and the American effort to repress it by force. The screen of falsehood which has been erected around the Tet Offensive in Hue was and is but another defense mechanism for the U.S. government and much of the American public as well to avoid dealing honestly with the real character of the struggle there.

3

American POWs Have Been Well Cared For

Jane Fonda

In 1972 Jane Fonda, daughter of actor Henry Fonda and the star of *Barefoot in the Park* (1967) and *Barbarella* (1968), traveled to North Vietnam to protest the American war. Along with her husband, Tom Hayden, who was one of the founders of Students for a Democratic Society (SDS) and who later became a California congressman, Fonda met with North Vietnamese officials, toured the countryside and the capital city of Hanoi, and expressed her solidarity with the people and regime of North Vietnam through several propaganda broadcasts on Radio Hanoi. While in Hanoi, Fonda was photographed visiting the crew of an antiaircraft gun used to fire at American planes; she also participated in a staged press conference with American prisoners of war (POWs), the purpose of which was to demonstrate that the prisoners were not being mistreated by the North Vietnamese. The following excerpt is a transcript of one of Jane Fonda's propaganda broadcasts from Hanoi. In this broadcast Fonda describes her meeting with the POWs and declares "they are all in good health." Upon returning to the United States, Fonda continued to claim that the POWs were being treated fairly and humanely; when returning POWs later described the torture they had endured at the hands of the North Vietnamese, Fonda called the returned prisoners "hypocrites and liars." As a result of her trip, her activities in North Vietnam, and her comments upon her return to the United States, Jane Fonda became known to thousands of veterans and Americans as "Hanoi Jane."

In the years following the end of the war Fonda continued her acting career, became a writer, and in the 1980s became fa-

Jane Fonda, radio address from Hanoi, Democratic Republic of Vietnam, August 15, 1972.

mous as a fitness guru and as the producer of mass-market exercise films. Fonda's trip to Vietnam continued to haunt her career, however, and in 1988 (after a film on which she was working was picketed by veterans) Fonda publicly apologized to veterans in an interview with journalist Barbara Walters on *20/20*. "I would like to say something, not just to Vietnam veterans in New England, but to men who were in Vietnam, who I hurt, or whose pain I caused to deepen because of things that I said or did," Fonda told Walters. "I was trying to help end the killing and the war, but there were times when I was thoughtless and careless about it and I'm . . . very sorry that I hurt them. And I want to apologize to them and their families." In 2005 Fonda released her autobiography, which is entitled *My Life So Far*.

This is Jane Fonda speaking from Hanoi. Yesterday evening, July 19, I had the opportunity of meeting seven U.S. pilots. Some of them were shot down as long ago as 1968 and some of them had been shot down very recently. They are all in good health. We had a very long talk, a very open and casual talk. We exchanged ideas freely. They asked me to bring back to the American people their sense of disgust of the war and their shame for what they have been asked to do.

American POWs Admit Guilt

They told me that the pilots believe they are bombing military targets. They told me that the pilots are told that they are bombing to free their buddies down below, but, of course, we all know that every bomb that falls on North Vietnam endangers the lives of the American prisoners.

They [the American POWs] asked me to bring back to the American people their sense of disgust of the war and their shame for what they have been asked to do.

They asked me: What can you do? They asked me to bring messages back home to their loved ones and friends, telling them to please be as actively involved in the peace movement as possible, to renew their efforts to end the war.

One of the men who has been in the service for many, many years has written a book about Vietnamese history, and I thought this was very moving, that during the time he's been here, and the time that he has had to reflect on what he has been through and what he has done to this country, he has—his thought has turned to this country, its history of struggle and the people that live here.

We All Want the War to End

They all assured me that they have been well cared for. They—they listen to the radio. They receive letters. They are in good health. They asked about news from home.

I think we all shared during the time that I spent with them a sense of—of deep sadness that a situation like this has to exist, and I certainly felt from them a very sincere desire to explain to the American people that this war is a terrible crime and that it must be stopped, and that Richard Nixon is doing nothing except escalating it while preaching peace, endangering their lives while saying he cares about the prisoners.

And I think one of the things that touched me the most was that one of the pilots said to me that he was reading a book called "The Draft," a book written by the American Friends Service Committee, and that in reading this book, he had understood a lot about what had happened to him as a human being in his 16 years of military service. He said that during those 16 years, he had stopped relating to civilian life, he had forgotten that there was anything else besides the military and he said in realizing what had happened to him, he was very afraid that this was happening to many other people.

I was very encouraged by my meeting with the pilots (because) I feel that the studying and the reading that they have been doing during their time here has taught them a great deal in putting the pieces of their lives back together again in a better way, hopefully, and I am sure that when—when they go home, they will go home better citizens than when they left.

4

The North Vietnamese Tortured Americans

Porter Halyburton

One of the great points at issue in discussion of the Vietnam War was whether the enemy—the North Vietnamese and the Vietcong guerrillas in the south—were innocent patriots victimized by the United States or rather evil and corrupt agents of a world Communist conspiracy. While the truth probably lies somewhere between these two extremes, prowar and antiwar activists at the time (and still today) tended to view and portray the North Vietnamese in these extreme ways. One way antiwar activists justified their antiwar feelings was by pointing out that even as Vietnamese hospitals and orphanages were being bombed, the captured American airmen responsible for such bombings were being treated well by the North Vietnamese. Actress and activist Jane Fonda famously traveled to North Vietnam and reported that American prisoners of war (POWs) were in good health and were not being tortured.

Whatever the rectitude of the North Vietnamese cause, however, and despite the rhetoric of antiwar activists such as Fonda, it is clear that American POWs were beaten, abused, and tortured by their North Vietnamese captors. In this article former U.S. Navy pilot Porter Halyburton talks with editor Christian G. Appy about his time as a POW. Halyburton discusses various war crimes committed against Americans and describes how in 1965 he was shot down over North Vietnam, was captured, and was tortured for information and confessions. Halyburton was held prisoner until 1973, when he returned to active service. He retired from the navy in 1984 as a

Porter Halyburton, *Patriots: The Vietnam War Remembered from All Sides.* New York: Viking, 2003. Copyright © 2003 by Christian G. Appy. Reproduced by permission of Viking Penguin, a division of Penguin Group (USA) Inc.

heavily decorated commander and became a professor of strategy at the U.S. Naval War College in Newport, Rhode Island.

[C]hristian G. Appy:] A professor of strategy, he is talking in his tidy, book-lined office at the Naval War College. A colleague interrupts to borrow a copy of Thucydides. The soft-spoken man from Davidson, North Carolina, picks up where he left off. He has the kind of calming voice you would gladly hear from the cockpit when the turbulence is bad. As the "back-seater" in a two-man Navy F-4 Phantom, his responsibilities included radar, navigation, and radio communications. In October 1965, on his seventy-fifth mission, his plane was shot down over North Vietnam. He was imprisoned until 1973.

Fighting the War from the Air

[Porter Halyburton:] More than half the missions I flew were at night. As we flew over the ocean from our aircraft carrier—the *Independence*—you could see all these lights. But as soon as they heard us coming they would sound an alarm, so by the time we got over land just about all the lights in the whole country would go out. Most of the time we were out looking for truck convoys going from north to south to connect to the Ho Chi Minh Trail [the main enemy supply route]. We were not very good at it. The Vietnamese were masters at camouflage. They put fresh-cut greenery over the top of trucks. They'd hear you coming and pull off the side of the road where they just looked like a clump of bushes.

We'd go out there with four Phantoms—fifteen million dollars' worth of airplanes—just looking for trucks on the road, and we weren't going to find them. So what do you do? You can't bring the bombs back, so you've got to find a place to get rid of them. Usually, you had to go to Tiger Island and just dump your bombs there. It was known to be heavily occupied by North Vietnamese troops and it was kind of a free-fire zone. I can't imagine how many tons and tons of ordnance we dropped on Tiger Island.

We were very frustrated that our targets were not very significant. If we bombed a bridge, three or four days later it was fixed, or they had constructed a ford. They also moved industries out into the jungles. And flying in the

North, we were very, very constrained. In the South, the B-52s [large Air Force bombers] would lay down a string of thousand-pound bombs and just completely devastate the entire area. But in the North, President Johnson said, "You're not going to bomb an out-house up there without my permission." The rules said we couldn't even attack a SAM [surface-to-air missile] site unless they launched a missile at us first. We had to send in somebody as bait to try to get them to fire a missile so we could attack the SAM sites. That kind of stuff really infuriated us.

Shot Down by the Enemy

Some places were very heavily defended. You just could not believe the barrage of antiaircraft fire. The day I got shot down, there were thirty-five airplanes in our flight. It was the largest strike of the war up until that time. Our target was a major bridge on the road that comes down from China to Hanoi. We were flying flak [antiaircraft fire] suppression. Our job was to use our rockets to fight it out with the antiaircraft sites and then the bombers were going to attack the bridge.

I saw the flak coming from the right. You don't hear anything, you just see the little black puffs. All of a sudden there was this thud. We took a hit right in the cockpit. The airplane was still flying level but I could see the pilot's helmet was gone. Papers were blowing all around the cockpit. I put my hand up to my oxygen mask and realized it was blown away. Then I looked down and saw a big piece of metal sticking out of my hand. I pulled that out and then pulled my ejection handle.

It happened so quickly. One minute you're sitting there and the next minute your parachute is opening. I could hear people shooting at me. I could hear bullets going through the canopy of the parachute. I landed pretty close to this village on the side of a little hill. There wasn't anyplace to hide. I tried to get away but I had a lot of gear on and my mouth just turned to cotton. I couldn't go full speed for long. When I had to stop and rest they pretty much surrounded me. They took my boots off and I had to walk barefoot to the village.

I have to tell a story about those boots. I went back to Vietnam last year and we went to the Army Museum. Inside this Plexiglas display case were these boots and you could see part of the name inside the boot. I leaned way over and there was my name! Those boots looked like they had been around. Somebody had obviously worn them for a while before they wound up in the museum.

I landed pretty close to this village on the side of a little hill. There wasn't anyplace to hide. I tried to get away but I had a lot of gear on and my mouth just turned to cotton.

Anyway, they took me back to the village, put me in a kind of animal shed, let me smoke cigarettes, brought me some water and a bowl of rice. After a couple of hours the army showed up in a jeep and we began our trip to Hanoi. They told me, "If you cooperate with us, and repent for your crimes, we will move you to a new camp, a really nice place. You'll be with all your friends. You'll have nice food and you can play games and write to your family. But if not, we'll move you to a worse place." Sure enough I was moved to the "Zoo."

I had nothing in there. It was completely dark. And yet at the top of the bricks there was a space of about three inches for ventilation that was covered with bars and shutters. One day I heard a noise up near the vent. I put my bed board up against the wall and climbed up to look. A tree had forced a leaf up between the shutters—a green leaf. I took that as a sign that no matter how isolated I was, God was somehow going to send me a sign.

Moved into a Worse Prison as Punishment

But I wouldn't cooperate so they moved me to an even worse place—a coal storage area. Ants, rats, mosquitoes by the ton. They would put my shitty little bowl of rice outside the door and leave it there for hours. By the time they finally gave it to me, it was completely covered with ants. It was inedible. I had dysentery by then and was getting disheartened. I hadn't talked to an American in months. The constant interrogation and indoctrination were wearing me down. I was about at the end of my rope and they're telling me again, "If you don't cooperate, we're going to move you to a worse place."

I said, "I don't see how you've got a worse place than this." That's when they moved me in with Fred Cherry. They said, "You must care for him. You must be his servant." I think they thought that would be the worst thing they could do—order a white guy to be a servant to this black guy. They very definitely tried to pit the two of us against each other, but it didn't take us long to become friends. I lived with Fred for eight months. He went through an awful time.

Fred had punched out of an F-105 [fighter aircraft] at about six hundred knots. His arm was just about ripped off and he had a broken foot. He couldn't do anything. They decided to operate on him and that's when his real troubles began. He was out of his mind with infection. Pus was dripping out of his cast. It was just horrible. He really couldn't do anything so I had to bathe him and feed him and help him go to the bucket. And I started really raising hell with the camp authorities to give him antibiotics.

Fred credits me with saving his life. I don't know about that, but I am certain that he turned my life around. When I moved in with him I said to myself, "God, this guy's in a lot worse shape than I am and he's not complaining." I had been out of touch with other people and was beginning to feel pretty sorry for myself. Taking care of Fred gave me a sense of purpose outside my own survival. It was very liberating. It was really the beginning of the idea that we were all in a brotherhood, all part of a big family. We would do anything for each other.

Beaten on a Propaganda March

On June 29, 1966, the United States bombed a target in Hanoi, an oil and lubricant storage area. The Vietnamese claimed we'd bombed civilian targets and all that kind of crap, as they always did. They launched this big propaganda campaign, and on July 6 sixty of us were marched through Hanoi, handcuffed in pairs. They told us we had to endure the anger of the Vietnamese people and show that we were repentant and bow our heads. Every time we raised our head we'd get hit on the back of the head with a rifle. So we started marching down the middle of the street and we had armed guards on either side. The crowds were lined up on the curbs. You could hear the Vietnamese guards prompting the crowds to yell slogans and chants. "Yankee imperialists! Air pirates! Murderers!"

The crowds got out of control and we were hammered. They pressed in and we got hit with mud, shoes, spit. That was really the only time during my captivity that I thought I probably was not going to make it. Even the guards were in a panic. Fortunately, they opened the gates to a stadium and we all kind of pushed in there and left most of the crowd outside. Then we went back to the prison.

Tortured for Information and Confessions

Right after that I was moved to a prison out in the country that was very primitive—"the Briarpatch"—and they began a systematic torture program to force us to write confessions. First, they just beat the crap out of you to soften you up. Or they made you sit on a little wooden stool for days. It became a gauge of your endurance. My limit was about three days before I collapsed from lack of sleep and food and water. We found out you could get a little water by faking sleep. They'd throw water on your face to wake you up and if you opened your mouth you could get a little swallow.

After that, the torture began. The method they used on me we called "max-cuffs." Your arms were pulled up behind your back and then they put these handcuffs on the upper part of your arm. Then they tied a rope on your wrists and pulled it up. I could actually see my fingertips over the top of my head when they did that. It pressed the nerves against the bone. It was like molten metal flowing through your veins—just indescribable pain.

> *So it soon became an official policy among American prisoners that we all had permission to give up after we had been tortured.*

They did that until they got the documents they wanted. One time it was for a confession, one time it was for biographical information, another time it was for a list of military missions. They did it repeatedly. It was much more difficult to refuse after you'd already given a certain kind of confession. The first time was the most devastating. I was in really bad shape. It was the middle of the night and if you wanted to speak to an interrogator or report anything you were supposed to say "*bao cao*" to the roving guard. It means "report."

I was yelling *"bao cao, bao cao,"* I was really in bad shape.

Psychologically, I think this was more damaging than the physical torture because you felt like you had completely failed. You had given up. You had capitulated. You had violated the code of conduct. You'd let everybody down. It was very depressing. Eventually I found out that everybody else, including the people I respected the most—like Jim Stockdale and Jerry Denton and Robert Risner—had been through exactly the same thing and had reacted pretty much the same way I did.

Fighting Back in an Unusual Way

At first we really tried to stick strictly to name, rank, service number, and date of birth. But it was a very unrealistic approach. You were taught that you should be willing to give up your life before saying anything more, but what if you can't kill yourself and they don't kill you? What if it's just continual, unbearable pain? We began to realize that nobody was successful in just saying no. Everybody had some physical limit. So it soon became an official policy among American prisoners that we all had permission to give up after we had been tortured. It almost sounds un-American but it was very practical. The ranking officers gave us guidance. You were to give up when you still had some mental acuity and could lie effectively. If you held out to the very end you'd have no mental skills at all. So you were supposed to accept some torture but it was okay to give up and make up some kind of cover story. We became adept at lying and covering up and using their ignorance of American customs and history and language and humor.

For example, the Vietnamese wanted to get evidence of war crimes to send to the Bertrand Russell war crimes tribunal in Stockholm. So they selected a navy F-4 crew to write a confession. They were tortured to do it and they wrote this confession. They had to confess to everything short of nuclear weapons—bombing schools, hospitals, civilians, dams, dikes, everything. And they had to give a list of people in their squadron. So they gave them the squadron roster and the Vietnamese took this off to Stockholm and read the list. The commander of the squadron was Dick Tracy and the other men included Clark Kent, and a whole bunch of other comic strip characters. This was an international embarrassment, because to force a POW to make a written statement is a war crime in itself, so they really indicted themselves. I think they finally figured out that we hated them enough that we would try to screw them at every opportunity.

The Situation Improved
When Ho Chi Minh Died

By 1969 I was living in the Zoo Annex in a room with eight other men. Shortly after Ho Chi Minh died in September of that year we began to see changes. I think they realized that torture hadn't worked very well and took Ho's death as an opportunity to change their policy. They hadn't really converted anybody and couldn't trust the stuff they forced from us. Also, Americans were making a big deal about our treatment, wearing POW bracelets and sending letters by the truckload to the Vietnamese delegation in Paris. I think the Vietnamese worried that this outcry might jeopardize the antiwar support they had nurtured so carefully.

They stopped taking us out for interrogations as much and the food improved. They added a meal—breakfast—a piece of bread with some grease and sugar on it. The cigarette ration was upped from three to six a day and they let us outside a bit more. Then we got to write and receive letters. The letter from my wife in 1970 was the first one in five years. But the biggest change was they quit torturing people.

They also built a special prison from the ground up that was to hold everybody. Compared to every other place it was pretty nice. There was even an area where they said they were going to put a Ping-Pong table and let us all out together during the daytime. But after we had been there a few months the Son Tay raid occurred.[1] After Son Tay they moved us all to the Hanoi Hilton [Hoa Lo Prison] and that ended a pretty good deal.

Security was tighter after Son Tay, but they didn't torture anyone on a regular basis, plus they kept us in big cells with forty or fifty people and we were so damn happy to be in a bigger group. During the years of solitary confinement we had communicated with other POWs using a tap code— tapping on the walls. During the time I was tortured I

1. On November 21, 1970, army rangers attempted to rescue U.S. POWs at Son Tay prison camp, about twenty miles northwest of Hanoi. The plan failed because the prisoners had been moved to another compound several months earlier.

mainly tapped on the wall with Howie Dunn, a marine F-4 pilot. I poured out my heart to him. We talked about what the Vietnamese were doing to us, we talked about food, we talked about women, we talked about our past lives and what we wanted to do in the future. We tapped for hours. At one point I said, "Howie, what do you look like?" He tapped back and said, "Actually, I look a lot like John Wayne." We were moved away from each other and I didn't talk to him for about five years. Right before we were coming home the Vietnamese allowed us to all get out together in a big compound and "greet one another" as they said. So I'm standing there talking to some people and this guy walks up to me—he's short and bald and nondescript, a complete and absolute stranger. I had never laid eyes on him before. He sticks out his hand and says, "Hi, I'm Howie Dunn." In a flash, there he was, my best friend.

[Appy:] After the war, he began hearing claims that some U.S. POWs had not been released by the Vietnamese and were still being held captive. "That really concerned me because we had tried so hard to make sure that didn't happen. We had memorized the name of every American in the North Vietnamese prison system, plus his rank, service, type of airplane, and date of shootdown. We thought we knew them all." Still, doubts nagged at him and in the early eighties he and some other ex-POWs pledged two million dollars to any Southeast Asian who brought out a genuine American POW. "News of this reward was disseminated over radio and by leaflet drops and plugged into every grapevine. Laos was filthy with people trying to sell phony bones and ID cards, but no one every produced a POW. That to me is as telling as anything that no POWs were left behind."

5

American POWs Were Never Mistreated

Ngoc Bao

The North Vietnamese did not leave it to American antiwar activists such as Jane Fonda to defend their regime against claims by former American prisoners of war (POWs) that the North Vietnamese had tortured captured American pilots. In this radio broadcast, which was entitled "Here Is Evidence of the Truth," and which was aired in Vietnamese by the state-run Hanoi radio on April 4, 1973, Ngoc Bao reported that American POWs had been treated with humanity and generosity. It was only after these POWs had returned to the United States and had been bribed with promotions, Bao explained, that they began to claim that they had been tortured. To prove that the POWs had been treated well, Bao played tapes in which captured American pilots "confessed" that they were part of a cruel and unjust war and reported that they were being cared for. The North Vietnamese actually extracted such "confessions" from POWs by beating and torturing them mercilessly.

Since the last U.S. aggressor pilots were released by our government, the U.S. Government—having pursued a policy of enmity against our people for a long time—has initiated a slanderous propaganda campaign to distort the truth and turn black into white in an attempt to deny our people's humane policy toward the captured U.S. POW's. The White House has exerted pressure on and bought the U.S. militarymen who had been allowed to enjoy our le-

Ngoc Bao, "Here is Evidence of the Truth," radio broadcast, April 4, 1973.

niency by summoning them separately and promoting many of them to higher ranks—forcing them to hold press conferences throughout the United States in order to slander our government and people. They have tried to cover the truth, describing our detention camps as hells on earth in the hope of generating a reaction of horror among the U.S. people. Taking advantage of this, the bellicose U.S. ruling clique has also attempted to sow suspicion between our government and people and the American progressives, the antiwar forces in the United States and the world peace movement that have over a long period displayed deep sympathy toward our people's anti-U.S. resistance. By these shameless acts, the White House has tried to erase its abominable crimes against our people, for which it has been condemned and despised by all mankind.

The Truth of What Happened

What, then, is the truth about what are termed tortures and cruel beatings suffered by U.S. POW's in our detention camps? Now let us listen to the voice of Denton, a U.S. Navy lieutenant commander captured on 18 July 1965 in Thanh Hoa: [Follows 2-minute mostly indistinct recorded statement attributed to POW Jeremiah A. Denton, Jr.]

The U.S. Government . . . has initiated a slanderous propaganda campaign to distort the truth and turn black into white in an attempt to deny our people's humane policy toward the captured U.S. POW's.

He committed the crime of using bombs to destroy Vietnamese hamlets and villages and kill innocent Vietnamese people. The Vietnamese people did not beat him upon his capture but gave him food and drinking water instead. He praised our penitentiary system filled with humanity and sternly criticized the U.S. Government's cruel war policy. He also asserted: The Vietnamese people have fought for a long time against aggression. In the (?anti-U.S.) war, Vietnam will eventually win even if it has to fight on for 20 more years, because the just cause belongs to Vietnam.

Nonetheless, after [U.S. president Richard] Nixon had

met Denton personally at the western White House, given him the rank of commander and promised he would soon propose to the U.S. Congress his promotion to the rank of general, Denton changed his tune. During a press conference at [word indistinct] college in North Carolina, he falsely accused us of treating him and his cohorts inhumanely and said that he had spent 4 consecutive years in solitary confinement. [James H.] Kasler, a U.S. Air Force major, is just like Denton. His crimes were not only against our people, since he had used bombs to destroy countless hamlets and villages and kill innumerable children of the fraternal Korean people. By these barbarous armed exploits, he was cited as a U.S. Air Force hero. On 29 June 1966 he had (?16) U.S. supersonic jets to conduct cruel attacks on an area northeast of Hanoi. Many of this cohorts paid for their crimes, but he escaped safely. He said: I thought that sooner or later I would be shot down (?upon approaching) Hanoi. His guess came true, but this time it was not approaching Hanoi. On 8 August 1966 he again led his cohorts to drop bombs on [words indistinct]. The bombs he dropped killed (?hundreds) of teachers and students at the mid-level pedagogy school in Yen Bai city. Many doctors and patients at the city hospital were also killed. The aircraft of the aggressor pilot Kasler (?was hit). He parachuted and broke a leg in landing.

> *The more it [the United States] distorts the truth, the more shining the truth about our people's humanity and generosity will become.*

When he was completely well again after treatment by our doctors, he said in a moving tone: [recorded statement in English fading into Vietnamese translation] We have caused great suffering to the Vietnamese people with our bombs and shells, but the militiamen capturing me treated me very well. My leg was broken; they tended the wound and gave me medical treatment with wholehearted care. They gave me adequate food and drink even though when looking into their eyes I knew they were very indignant toward me. I fortunately have many times witnessed the great suffering caused by our bombing to the Vietnamese people. These are extremely cruel acts conducted by our government. In short, I would like to thank the DRV [Democratic Republic of Vietnam, North Vietnamese] people for their humane treatment toward me and I beg the Vietnamese people to forgive my criminal acts and allow me to enjoy a policy of leniency.

Former POWs Are Bribed to Lie

This is Kasler's statement after his receipt of our doctors' kindness. But now, after being promoted by Nixon from major to colonel, he has turned ungrateful to our people. Dazed by the fame and wealth bestowed by Nixon, he has shut his eyes and falsely accused us of treating him very brutally and torturing him.

The shameless ruling clique in the United States will spend its efforts in vain in fabricating such ridiculous scenes. The more it distorts the truth, the more shining the truth about our people's humanity and generosity will become. The American progressives have continued and will continue to spit on its farce of turning black into white. Jane Fonda, a famous U.S. movie star, asserted: Anyone who distorts the truth will be sternly judged by history. Captain (Willinger), a captured U.S. pilot whom we released, told the truth in saying that his protest against the U.S. Government and demand that the U.S. Congress use the law to end the war in Vietnam had been made of his own volition without anyone forcing him.

Most recently on 1 April U.S. Air Force Col Walter Wilber valiantly declared on CBS, an American television company, that during almost 5 years of detention in North Vietnam, he had never been ill-treated as disclosed by a number of returned U.S. POW's. This is certainly the truth and people with good sense will continue to speak out this truth.

Glossary

ARVN: Army of the Republic of Vietnam, the military of South Vietnam.

free-fire zones: Designated areas in which South Vietnamese (**ARVN**) or American forces were free to attack on sight any suspected targets or any humans, whether they were soldiers, civilians, men, women, or children. Non–**Vietcong** residents of these areas were urged to move to "strategic hamlets," which were villages protected by South Vietnamese government troops.

Hamburger Hill: More properly called Ap Bia Mountain or Hill 937, a hill in the A Shau Valley that in 1969 was the scene of one of the bloodiest battles of the conflict. The battle, in which 56 Americans were killed and 420 were wounded, was seen by the American people as so bloody and so pointless that President Richard Nixon was forced to end major ground combat operations in Vietnam.

Khe Sanh: An isolated American base near the border between South Vietnam and Laos. In 1968 it became the site of an internationally famous siege when it was surrounded by units of the **PAVN**. Two hundred five marines were killed in the siege, while the North Vietnamese lost between ten thousand and fifteen thousand soldiers.

My Lai: Small villages in South Vietnam, one of which (My Lai IV) was the site of a massacre in March 1968 of over three hundred unarmed Vietnamese men, women, and children by U.S. troops. The incident became public in the fall of 1969 and led to the courts-martial of Lieutenant William F. Calley and some of his subordinates.

NLF: National Liberation Front, or National Front for the Liberation of Southern Vietnam. The organization that led guerrilla resistance against the French in Vietnam and, later, against the Americans and the South Vietnamese gov-

134 Vietnam War Crimes

ernment. **NLF** military forces were known to the Americans as the **Vietcong**.

NVA: North Vietnamese Army, the military force of the country of North Vietnam. The **NVA** and the **PAVN** were the same force and did not include the **Vietcong** or the **Vietminh**.

Operation Phoenix: A covert joint operation of the CIA, the U.S. military, and South Vietnamese forces to identify or assassinate key **Vietcong** officials in South Vietnam. It was later the subject of congressional hearings.

PAVN: People's Army of Vietnam, the term North Vietnam used to refer to its military forces; the same forces were referred to by the Americans as the **NVA**. The **PAVN/NVA** did not include the **Vietcong**.

search and destroy: A strategy in the Vietnam conflict conceived by General William Westmoreland, who at the time was the commander of all U.S. forces in Vietnam. Under this strategy, the military sent out numerous small patrols to find the enemy and call in heavy artillery and air support to destroy the forces discovered.

Vietcong: Short for *Viet Nam Cong San*, or Vietnamese Communists, the guerrillas in the south who fought the South Vietnamese government. The **Vietcong** were different from the **NVA/PAVN** troops, who were regular army soldiers rather than guerrilla fighters.

Vietminh: Short for *Viet Nam Doc Lap Dong Minh Hoi*, League for the Independence of Vietnam. A group formed in 1941 to seek Vietnamese independence from France and to oppose the Japanese presence during World War II. It led North Vietnam after the French withdrawal in 1954.

VVA: Vietnam Veterans of America, a national organization founded in 1978 to support Vietnam-era veterans and their families.

VVAW: Vietnam Veterans Against the War, founded in 1967 to channel the antiwar feelings of those who had served in Vietnam. The VVAW sponsored the Winter Soldier investigation of 1971 and chose John Kerry as its spokesman to testify to the Senate Foreign Relations Committee in April 1971 about problems with the war in Vietnam.

For Further Research

Background and General History

Christian G. Appy, *Patriots: The Vietnam War Remembered from All Sides.* New York: Viking, 2003.

Bernard Edelman, ed., *Dear America: Letters Home from Vietnam.* New York: Norton, 1985.

George C. Herring, *America's Longest War: The United States and Vietnam, 1950–1975,* 3rd ed. New York: McGraw-Hill, 1996.

Guenter Lewy, *America in Vietnam.* Oxford, England: Oxford University Press, 1978.

Myra MacPherson, *Long Time Passing: Vietnam and the Haunted Generation.* New York: Doubleday, 1984.

John Norton Moore and Robert F. Turner, *The Real Lessons of the Vietnam War: Reflections Twenty-Five Years After the Fall of Saigon.* Durham, NC: Carolina Academic Press, 2002.

U.S. Politics and Policy

Noam Chomsky, *Rethinking Camelot: JFK, the Vietnam War, and U.S. Political Culture.* Boston: South End, 1993.

David Halberstam, *The Best and the Brightest.* 1972. Reprint, New York: Vintage Books, 1996.

Robert S. McNamara with Brian Vandemark, *In Retrospect: The Tragedy and Lessons of Vietnam.* New York: Random House, 1995.

War Crimes and Atrocities

Roy Gutman and David Rieff, eds., *Crimes of War: What the Public Should Know.* New York: Norton, 1999.

Michael Howard, George Andreopoulos, and Mark Shulman, eds., *The Laws of War: Constraints on Warfare in the Western World.* New Haven, CT: Yale University Press, 1997.

Michael Reisman, *The Laws of War: A Comprehensive Collection of Primary Documents on International Laws Governing Armed Conflict*. New York: Vintage, 1994.

Donald A. Wells, *War Crimes and Laws of War*. Lanham, MD: University Press of America, 1984.

American War Crimes

Mark Baker, *Nam: The Vietnam War in the Words of the Men and Women Who Fought There*. New York: Morrow, 1981.

John Duffett and Bertrand Russell, *Against the Crime of Silence: Proceedings of the Russell International War Crimes Tribunal: Stockholm, Copenhagen*. New York: O'Hare Books and Bertrand Russell Peace Foundation, 1968.

Erwin Knoll and Judith Nies McFadden, *War Crimes and the American Conscience*. New York: Holt, Rinehart & Winston, 1970.

Vietnam Veterans Against the War, *The Winter Soldier Investigation: An Inquiry into American War Crimes*. Boston: Beacon, 1972.

The My Lai Massacre

Michal R. Belknap, *The Vietnam War on Trial: The My Lai Massacre and the Court-Martial of Lieutenant Calley*. Lawrence: University Press of Kansas, 2002.

Michael Bilton and Kevin Sim, *Four Hours in My Lai*. New York: Viking, 1992.

William L. Calley with John Sack, *Lieutenant Calley: His Own Story*. New York: Tempo, 1974.

Seymour M. Hersh, *My Lai 4: A Report on the Massacre and Its Aftermath*. New York: Random House, 1970.

Vietnamese War Crimes

Stephane Courtois et al., *The Black Book of Communism: Crimes, Terror, Repression*. Cambridge, MA: Harvard University Press, 1999.

John G. Hubbell, *P.O.W.: A Definitive History of the American Prisoner-of-War Experience in Vietnam, 1964–1973*. New York: Reader's Digest, 1976.

Douglas Pike, *Viet Cong: The Organization and Technique of the National Liberation Front of South Vietnam.* Cambridge, MA: MIT Press, 1966.

Stuart I. Rochester and Frederick Kiley, *Honor Bound: American Prisoners of War in Southeast Asia, 1961–1973.* Annapolis, MD: Naval Institute Press, 1999.

Web Sites

Veterans History Project, www.loc.gov. The Veterans History Project of the American Folklife Center at the Library of Congress collects and preserves the wartime memories of American veterans and civilians. Researchers can search though and download an ever-growing number of interviews and oral histories.

Vietnam War Bibliography, www.clemson.edu. This online bibliography, compiled and maintained by Clemson University history professor Edwin E. Moïse, lists more than four thousands items, with direct links to the online texts of several hundred articles and books.

The Virtual Vietnam Archive, www.vietnam.ttu.edu. The Vietnam Project at Texas Tech University has become a vitally important center for the study of the Vietnam conflict. The Project's Virtual Vietnam Archive contains an enormous wealth of material, including almost 2 million pages of scanned documents available online.

Index